SpringerBriefs in Anthropology

SpringerBriefs in Anthropology presents concise summaries of cutting-edge research and practical applications in all aspects of Anthropology. Featuring compact volumes of 85 to 125 pages, the series covers a range of content from professional to academic. Typical topics might include: a snapshot of a hot or emerging topic, a contextual literature review, timely report of state-of-the art analytical techniques, in-depth case study, presentation of core concepts that students must understand in order to make independent contributions. Briefs allow authors to present their ideas and readers to absorb them with minimal time investment. Briefs will be published as part of Springer's eBook collection, with millions of users worldwide. In addition, Briefs will be available for individual print and electronic purchase. Briefs are characterized by fast, global electronic dissemination, standard publishing contracts, easy-to-use manuscript preparation and formatting guidelines, and expedited production schedules. We aim for publication 8-12 weeks after acceptance. Both solicited and unsolicited manuscripts are considered for publication in this series. Briefs can also arise from the scale up of a planned chapter. Instead of simply contributing to an edited volume, the author gets an authored book with the space necessary to provide more data, fundamentals and background on the subject, methodology, future outlook, etc. SpringerBriefs in Anthropology contain a number of distinct subseries focusing Anthropology and Ethics, Human Behavior and Biology, and Human Ecology. Please see the webpages for each subseries for a more precise description of each.

More information about this series at http://www.springer.com/series/11496

Francis Müller

Design Ethnography

Epistemology and Methodology

Francis Müller
Zurich University of the Arts
Zurich, Switzerland

Translated by
Anna Brailovsky
NA
Los Angeles, CA, USA

ISSN 2195-0806　　　　　　ISSN 2195-0814　(electronic)
SpringerBriefs in Anthropology
ISBN 978-3-030-60395-3　　ISBN 978-3-030-60396-0　(eBook)
https://doi.org/10.1007/978-3-030-60396-0

This book is an open access publication

© The Author(s) 2021
Open Access This book is licensed under the terms of the Creative Commons Attribution 4.0 International License (http://creativecommons.org/licenses/by/4.0/), which permits use, sharing, adaptation, distribution and reproduction in any medium or format, as long as you give appropriate credit to the original author(s) and the source, provide a link to the Creative Commons license and indicate if changes were made.
The images or other third party material in this book are included in the book's Creative Commons license, unless indicated otherwise in a credit line to the material. If material is not included in the book's Creative Commons license and your intended use is not permitted by statutory regulation or exceeds the permitted use, you will need to obtain permission directly from the copyright holder.
The use of general descriptive names, registered names, trademarks, service marks, etc. in this publication does not imply, even in the absence of a specific statement, that such names are exempt from the relevant protective laws and regulations and therefore free for general use.
The publisher, the authors, and the editors are safe to assume that the advice and information in this book are believed to be true and accurate at the date of publication. Neither the publisher nor the authors or the editors give a warranty, expressed or implied, with respect to the material contained herein or for any errors or omissions that may have been made. The publisher remains neutral with regard to jurisdictional claims in published maps and institutional affiliations.

This Springer imprint is published by the registered company Springer Nature Switzerland AG.
The registered company address is: Gewerbestrasse 11, 6330 Cham, Switzerland

Acknowledgement

This book is an abridged version of *Designethnografie. Methodologie und Praxisbeispiele* [Design Ethnography: Methods and Practice], which was published by the Social Science division of Springer Verlag (Germany/Wiesbaden) in 2018. I would like to take the opportunity to thank Springer Nature Switzerland for making this English edition possible and for their productive and enjoyable collaboration. Particular thanks are due to Anna Brailovsky for the translation of the text.

Zurich/Mexico City   Francis Müller

Contents

1	**Introduction: Design as a Discipline of Alternation**	1
	References	4
2	**The Blind Spot**	7
	2.1 The Incorporation of Everyday Knowledge	9
	References	11
3	**The Everyday World and Intersubjectivity**	13
	3.1 Symbolic Interaction and the Generalized Other	15
	3.2 Professional Indifference and Lack of Moral Judgment	17
	References	18
4	**Design Research: Immersion and Intervention**	21
	4.1 Warm, Involving, and Risky	23
	4.2 Research Through Design	24
	4.3 Contingency and Serendipity	26
	References	27
5	**Methods and Aspects of Field Research**	31
	5.1 The Foreign Worlds Next Door and Defamiliarization	32
	5.2 Focused Ethnographies and Design Anthropology	34
	5.3 Access to the Field	37
	5.4 Researcher's Role in the Field	39
	5.5 Observation	40
	5.6 Dimensions of Observation	41
	5.7 Front and Back Regions	42
	5.8 Interviews and Conversations	45
	5.9 Narrative Interview	46
	5.10 Ethnographic Interviews	47
	5.11 The Senses	48
	5.12 Things and Material Culture	50
	5.13 Consumption Is Not Superficial	51
	5.14 The Contingency of Things	53

	5.15	Field Notes...	53
	5.16	Sketches and Illustrations.............................	54
	5.17	Photography and Video................................	55
	5.18	Factors that Influence Production of Visual Data.........	57
	5.19	Participant Produced Images...........................	58
	5.20	Digital Ethnography...................................	59
	5.21	Participatory Action Research..........................	61
	5.22	Participatory Photography and Cultural Probes...........	62
	5.23	Photo Elicitation.....................................	64
	5.24	Interventions..	65
	5.25	Withdrawing from the Field............................	66
	5.26	Ethics...	67
	References...		68
6	**Analysis**...		77
	6.1	Transcriptions.......................................	78
	6.2	Grounded Theory.....................................	79
	6.3	Ethnosemantic Analysis...............................	80
	6.4	Structured and Narrative Interviews.....................	81
	6.5	Computer-Based Analysis..............................	82
	6.6	Visual Data..	82
	6.7	Things and Material Culture...........................	84
	References...		85
7	**Representation and Reporting**............................		87
	References...		89
8	**Epilogue**...		91
	References...		92

About the Author

Francis Müller works as lecturer for design ethnography and sociology in the subject area Trends & Identity in the Design Department, Zurich University of the Arts (ZHdK), Switzerland. He also has lectureships in the School of Humanities and Social Sciences of University St. Gallen (HSG) and in universities in Mexico and Chile.

Chapter 1
Introduction: Design as a Discipline of Alternation

Abstract Design is never creating out of nothing—it always has specific cultural points of reference. Design alters and adapts, whereby the discipline always takes what exists as a reference point, which also makes it heretical. Design requires and generates knowledge, because designers always need to engage with specific lifeworlds. Through methods such as ethnography, this knowledge can be made explicit, which makes the discipline of design capable of connecting with other academic disciplines. Ethnography in the context of design differs from ethnography in the social sciences: it is quicker and embedded in the iterative processes that designing involves.

Keywords Alternation · Design · Ethnography · Knowledge · Research

The use of the term "Design" is today downright inflated. A Google search for it immediately returns 25,270,000,000 entries.[1] It is associated, among other things, with beautiful furnishings, flashy fingernails, cars, sneakers, and sex toys. It can also refer to systems, events, interfaces, and processes. The term can be traced back to the Latin *designare*, which led to the Italian *disegnare*, which initially meant *to describe* and later came to mean *to draft*. From an anthropological perspective, design is an expression of appreciation for the new: It is neither manual skill nor handicraft, in which artifacts are produced through the replication of traditional manufacturing techniques. Tradition may well be an important point of reference, since design never creates from nothing (Latour 2008, p. 5), but design does alter traditions, however. It is a heretical discipline—a discipline of transformation, to which Bruno Latour even ascribes revolutionary powers (2008, p. 2).

Design requires and at the same time generates knowledge. Designers create things or systems that are later used by people about whose lifeworlds or *native point view* they know very little (Blomberg et al. 1993, p. 141 ff.). Accordingly, they assimilate project-specific knowledge. Claudia Mareis describes design as a

---
[1] Accessed 26 May 2019.

© The Author(s) 2021
F. Müller, *Design Ethnography*, SpringerBriefs in Anthropology,
https://doi.org/10.1007/978-3-030-60396-0_1

"knowledge culture" (2011). Designers incorporate stores of implicit knowledge through their practice, which they often do not reflect upon (Mareis 2010, p. 126 ff.; Schön 1983, p. 51 ff.). The consequence is an intuitive approach to design that is guided by internalized experiential knowledge. This knowledge remains bound to the individual, or at best, to the social environment with which they interact (Mareis 2010, p. 125). If design is to become an accessible knowledge culture capable of *connectivity* then it must free itself of its dependency on the individual.

Design is situated within a diverse field of disciplines that influence it (Götz 2010, p. 55 f.): Engineering, natural sciences, sociology, anthropology, psychology, economics—to name just a few. At the same time, design is not an academic discipline, even if there have been efforts to establish it as such (which incidentally has given rise to some heated debate). The thesis of this book is that the frequently implicit knowledge of design must be made explicit. This will allow design to make connections to other disciplines (Milev 2011, p. 46; Schultheis 2005, p. 68). Articulating and reflecting upon design knowledge strengthens the position of design. Since design is still a practice, however, it cannot become a scientific discipline in a true sense. At issue, rather, is the fact that design is a discipline of exploration and inquiry. Design should understand its own generation of knowledge as "reflection in action" (Schön 1983, p. 76 ff.). This requires methods: a term that goes back to the ancient Greek word for "pursuit." Methods such as ethnography are procedures that should not simply be applied dogmatically, but rather are meant to lead to reflection about one's own actions. It is only when these procedures are explicitly articulated that it becomes possible to consciouly adapt and transform them.

The term ethnography also goes back to ancient Greek and means someting like "description of a foreign people." It was not until the late nineteenth and early twentieth centuries that ethnography became a method of cultural sociology and social anthropology. Ethnography presupposes foreignness—lack of familiarity between the ethnographer and the people and lifeworlds they investigate. This suggests that ethnography is actually a common practice in design research: As soon as designers leave the libraries and the on-line databases to enter the field—and they must!—they are ethnographically active. Every observation of an everyday situation, no matter how trivial, that is made in the course of a design project is already a simple form of ethnography. This occurs often without any awareness that a research method is already being used.

It should be noted, however, that ethnography is not an academic discipline, but a method situated in various (partly academic and partly applied) disciplines—cultural sociology; social and cultural anthropology; organizational science; business administration; development aid; pedagogy; art; gender, cultural, and queer studies; and of course design. Ethnography has been adapted in each of these disciplines. Design ethnography is accordingly also grounded in cultural-sociological and socio-anthropological approaches (Gunn et al. 2013; Milev 2013), though these are adapted in rather design-specific ways. While in cultural sociology and social anthropology, ethnography happens through long-term immersion in foreign lifeworlds, design ethnographies are often of far shorter duration—as in other applied disciplines—due to time constraints. Such approaches are known as "quick and dirty ethnography" (Hughes et al. 1994, p. 433 ff.; Knoblauch 2001, p. 128; Plowman 2003, p. 34), "short-term ethnography" (Pink and Morgan 2013), "rapid ethnography" (Norman 1999), and of course, "design ethnography" (Crabtree et al. 2012; Nova 2014; Müller 2018; Salvador et al. 1999). Corresponding approaches have emerged in the Anglo-Saxon world in the context of workplace studies (Knoblauch 2000; Knoblauch and Heath 1999; Suchman 1987), in which anthropological methods have been combined with engineering and technical sciences to investigate workplace situtations that have been transformed by technological innovations.

Ethnography is a more complex, unstructured, and chaotic process than scientific research. It is an experiential, explorative research method in which the physical presence and sensory experience of the researcher play a part as they move corporeally (apart from on-line ethnographies) through other realities (Goffman 1989, p. 125). For the "empirical world must forever be the central point of concern" (Blumer 1986, p. 22).

This book is an attempt to shed light on design ethnography at the epistemological and methodological level. In this endeavor, design ethnography is not understood as a self-contained method, but rather as a starting point for opening up new perspectives and thinking about new methods that lead in iterative steps to the creation of form. Such processes can certainly also lead to discontinuities that are inherent to research. For those who know from the start what they are looking for observe their field of investigation through tunnel vision. If a research project is guided from the beginning by hypotheses that do not change during the process, then this prevents true exploration from taking place (Malinowski 1932, p. 16 f.). That is why research is genuinely risky (Latour 1998, p. 208): One leaves one's comfort zone, which can occasionally shake one's own worldview. The "art" consists of reflecting on and mapping these processes and constructing from them a "mosaic" (Prus 1997, p. 27 ff.) of the reality under investigation.

The world cannot be observed neutrally from a box seat, especially since the observer is always themselves situated in it (Maturana and Varela 2003, p. 5 ff.; Denzin 2014, p. 70 f.; Haraway 1988). Realization does not occur passively and objectively, in the way the natural sciences suggest. It is the natural sciences in particular that exhibit a highly constructed character (Dellwing and Prus 2012, p. 206): The laboratory, the measuring instruments, etc., are constructed and man-made. A certain style of thinking manifests itself in them (Fleck 1986, p. 147 ff.). They are not neutral. Rather, they are cultural constructions—just like the idea of objectivity, which originated in Western philosophy of science and is not an anthropological constant. For man is "an animal suspended in webs of significance he himself has spun" (Geertz 1973, p. 5). The sciences are part of this man-made culture.

While scientific research obscures its own constructed character behind an ethos of objectivity, design ethnography can and should expose it. It does not need to strive for objectivity. Its methods are not applied dogmatically but playfully. They can be adapted, varied, and transcended on a case-by-case basis and situationally. This does not, however, mean it is completely arbitrary: The methods must be reflected upon and made explicit, at least if design research is to become compatible with other disciplines. The aim, then, is not to imitate the natural sciences proper, but rather to arrive at interesting and surprising findings through playful ethnographic methods.

While in social science research, ethnography is usually concerned with investigating "natural" situations—that is, situations that have not been prompted by the researcher (Dellwing and Prus 2012, p. 54 ff.)—design is interested in disturbing such "natural" situations: It intervenes, it gives form, it is "research through design" (Findeli 2004, p. 44). Giving form thus takes on an epistemic quality (Ammon and Froschauer 2013, p. 16), which makes visible *design-specific modes of knowledge*. Such modes consist in quick, iterative processes in which a sharp line cannot always be drawn between investigation and form-giving. This is confirmed in a statement by the Chilean epistemologists Humberto R. Maturana and Francisco L. Varela, who wrote that every action is a realization and every realization an action (2003, p. 13).

References

Ammon, S., & Froschauer, E. M. (2013). Zur Einleitung: Wissenschaft Entwerfen. Perspektiven einer reflexiven Entwurfsforschung [An introduction: Designing science. Perspectives of reflexive design research]. In S. Ammon & E. M. Froschauer (Eds.), *Wissenschaft Entwerfen: Vom forschenden Entwerfen zur Entwurfsforschung der Architektur* [Designing science: From researching design to design research in architecture] (pp. 15–44). Munich: Wilhelm Fink.

Blomberg, J., Giacomi, J., Mosher, A., & Swenton-Wall, P. (1993). Ethnographic field methods and their relation to design. In D. Schuler & A. Namioka (Eds.), *Participatory design: Principles and practices* (pp. 123–155). Hillsdale, NJ: Lawrence Erlbaum.

Blumer, H. (1986). *Symbolic interactionism. Perspective and method.* Berkeley: University of California Press.

Crabtree, A., Roucefield, M., & Tolmie, P. (2012). *Doing design ethnography.* London: Springer.

Dellwing, M., & Prus, R. (2012). *Einführung in die interaktionistische Ethnografie. Soziologie im Außendienst* [Introduction to interactionist ethnography: Sociology in the field]. Wiesbaden: Springer VS.

Denzin, N. K. (2014). *Interpretative autoethnography.* London: Sage.

Findeli, A. (2004). *Die projektgeleitete Forschung. Eine Methode der Designforschung* [Project-led research: A method of design research]. Swiss Design Network Symposium. HGK Basel, pp. 41–51. Retrieved May 11, 2017, from http://swissdesignnetwork.ch/src/publication/erstesdesignforschungssymposium-2004/ErstesDesignForschungssymposium_2004.pdf

Fleck, L. (1986). To look, to see, to know. In R. S. Cohen & T. Schnelle (Eds.), *Cognition and fact: Materials on Ludwik Fleck.* Dordrecht: Springer. https://doi.org/10.1007/978-94-009-4498-5.

Geertz, C. (1973). *The interpretation of cultures.* New York: Basic Books.

Goffman, E. (1989). On fieldwork. *Journal of Contemporary Ethnography, 18,* 123–132.

Götz, M. (2010). Design als Abenteuer [Design as adventure]. In F. Romero-Tejedor & W. Jonas (Eds.), *Positionen zur Designwissenschaft* [Positions in design science] (pp. 53–57). Kassel: University Press.

Gunn, W., Otto, T., & Smith, R. C. (2013). *Design anthropology: Theory and practice.* London: Bloomsbury.

References

Haraway, D. (1988). Situated knowledges: The science question in feminism and the privilege of partial perspective. *Feminist Studies, 14*(3), 575–599.

Hughes, J., King, V., Rodden, T., & Andersen, H. (1994). Moving out of the control room: Ethnography in system design. In R. Futura & C. Neuwirth (Eds.), *Transcending boundaries: Proceedings of the conference on computer supported cooperative work* (pp. 429–439). New York: ACM.

Knoblauch, H. (2000). Workplace Studies und Video: Zur Entwicklung der visuellen Ethnographie von Technologie und Arbeit [Workplace studies and video: on the development of the visual ethnography of technology and work]. In I. Götz & A. Wittel (Eds.), *Arbeitskulturen im Umbruch: Zur Ethnografie der Arbeit und Organisation* [Work cultures in transition: On the ethnography of work and organization] (pp. 159–174). Berlin: Waxmann.

Knoblauch, H. (2001). Fokussierte Ethnographie [Focused ethnography]. *Sozialer Sinn* [Social sense], *1*, 123–141.

Knoblauch, H., & Heath, C. (1999). Technologie, Interaktion und Organisation: die Workplace-Studies [Technology, interaction and organization: The workplace studies]. *Schweizerische Zeitschrift für Soziologie* [Swiss Journal of Sociology], *25*(2), 163–181.

Latour, B. (1998). From the world of science to the world of research? *Science, 280*, 208–209.

Latour, B. (2008). A cautious Prometheus? A few steps toward a philosophy of design (with special attention to Peter Sloterdijk). In *Proceedings of the 2008 annual International Conference of the Design History Society—Falmouth, 3–6 September 2009.* Retrieved July 15, 2019, from http://www.bruno-latour.fr/sites/default/files/112-DESIGN-CORNWALL-GB.pdf

Malinowski, B. (1932). *Argonauts of the Western Pacific*. London: George Routledge & Sons.

Mareis, C. (2010). The nature of design. In C. Mareis, G. Joost, & K. Kimpel (Eds.), *Entwerfen—Wissen—Produzieren. Designforschung im Nwendungskontext* [Design—knowledge—production: Design research in an application context] (pp. 121–143). Bielefeld: Transcript.

Mareis, C. (2011). *Design als Wissenskultur. Interferenzen zwischen Design- und Wissensdiskursen seit 1960* [Design as a culture of knowledge: Interferences between design and knowledge discourses since 1960]. Bielefeld: Transcript.

Maturana, H. R., & Varela, F. J. (2003). *El árbol del conocimiento. Las bases biológicas del entendimiento humano* [The tree of knowledge: The biological basis of human understanding]. Buenos Aires: Lumen.

Milev, Y. (2011). *Emergency Design. Anthropotechniken des Über/Lebens* [Emergency design: Anthropotechnics of survival]. Berlin: Merve.

Milev, Y. (2013). *D.A.: A transdisciplinary handbook of design anthropology*. Frankfurt: Peter Lang.

Müller, F. (2018). *Designethnografie: Methodologie und Praxisbeispiele* [Design ethnography: Methodology and practical examples]. Wiesbaden: Springer VS.

Norman, D. A. (1999). Rapid ethnography. In H. Aldersey-Williams, J. Bound, & R. Coleman (Eds.), *The method lab: User research for design* (pp. 24–25). London: Design for Aging Network (DAN), Royal College of Art.

Nova, N. (2014). *Beyond design ethnography: How designers practice ethnographic research*. Geneva: SHS & HEAD.

Pink, S., & Morgan, J. (2013). Short-term ethnography: Intense routes to knowing. *Symbolic Interaction, 36*(3), 351–361.

Plowman, T. (2003). Ethnography and critical design practice. In B. Laurel (Ed.), *Design research: Methods and perspectives* (pp. 30–38). Cambridge, MA: MIT Press.

Prus, R. (1997). *Subcultural mosaic and intersubjective realities: An ethnographic research agenda for pragmatizing the social sciences*. Albany, NY: State University of New York Press.

Salvador, T., Bell, G., & Anderson, K. (1999). Design ethnography. *Design Management Journal, 10*(4), 35–41. https://doi.org/10.1111/j.1948-7169.1999.tb00274.x.

Schön, D. A. (1983). *The reflexive practitioner: How professionals think in action*. New York: Basic Books.

Schultheis, F. (2005). Disziplinierung des Designs [Disciplining of design]. In *Forschungslandschaften im Umfeld des Designs* [Research landscapes in the design setting] (pp. 65–84). Zurich: Swiss Design Network.

Suchman, L. A. (1987). *Plans and situated actions: The problem of human-machine communication*. Cambridge: Cambridge University Press.

Open Access This chapter is licensed under the terms of the Creative Commons Attribution 4.0 International License (http://creativecommons.org/licenses/by/4.0/), which permits use, sharing, adaptation, distribution and reproduction in any medium or format, as long as you give appropriate credit to the original author(s) and the source, provide a link to the Creative Commons license and indicate if changes were made.

The images or other third party material in this chapter are included in the chapter's Creative Commons license, unless indicated otherwise in a credit line to the material. If material is not included in the chapter's Creative Commons license and your intended use is not permitted by statutory regulation or exceeds the permitted use, you will need to obtain permission directly from the copyright holder.

Chapter 2
The Blind Spot

Abstract In our everyday world, we operate within a reality that we experience as "normal," and which we do not question further, although it is actually man-made and designed. In design ethnography, however, we need to define this reality not simply as given, but as constructed and contingent. We need to make blind spots visible and decompose the reality that we classify on the basis of received knowledge in a phenomenological way, which is epistemologically relevant. We must deliberately alienate ourselves from the familiar in order to seek new connections of meaning in it.

Keywords Classification · Ensemble · Everyday knowledge · Gaze · Phenomenology

In October 1974, the French writer George Perec set himself down for 3 days in a café at the Place Saint-Suplice in Paris, where he observed the goings-on and made notes. In his *Attempt at Exhausting a Place in Paris* (2010), he records among other things: "Asphalt," "Some sort of basset hound," "Human beings," "Bread (baguette)" (2010, p. 6). He does not see the square as an ensemble or the bus as a means of transportation; rather he sees individual living beings, things, and signs. He doesn't comment, doesn't interpret. His intention consists in describing "[...] that which is generally not taken note of, that which is not noticed, that which has no importance: what happens when nothing other happens than the weather, people, cars, and clouds" (2010, p. 3). Perec inventories the things and people of everyday reality. He wants to suspend the certainties with which we classify everyday reality. Of course, this can only go so far, especially since Perec does speak of "cars" and not of colorful metal shells moving forward on wheels (and even this description is based on an arbitrary language). It is thus accurate to speak of an *attempt*, and in particular of a phenomenological one—that is, one that investigates reality as it reveals itself to us aesthetically—and not an ontological one. It is of course not as if Perec leaves Plato's cave by means of his experiment; rather, he is simply sitting in a café and playing just a little bit with the reality that presents itself to us.

© The Author(s) 2021
F. Müller, *Design Ethnography*, SpringerBriefs in Anthropology,
https://doi.org/10.1007/978-3-030-60396-0_2

Even if Perec seems like a purely passive observer, he is active. He may not be altering what is happening on the square, but what happens alters him. By shifting his gaze and seeing "other" things, or seeing the same things differently, he deliberately perceives the world differently. Perec is not simply a visitor to the café; he is an observer, an author. He lingers in the café to write a literary text. His gaze is open and paradoxically intentional at the same time: by seeing something, he does not see something else. Seeing always produces "blind spots" (Maturana and Varela 2003, p. 13). Perec demonstrates that we do not necessarily need to travel to the Amazon in order to enter another world. A visit to the nearest café on a square in our familiar city, a pen, a notebook, and some time are sufficient. The other, strange world is here. We are in its midst.

By putting his observations into written form, Perec draws on a pre-fabricated language that classifies through naming (Strauss 2017, p. 17 ff.). Thus Perec brings forth a world through language: an experimental literary text; a text of the OuLiPo movement. At the same time, his text has an epistemic quality. Perec recognizes something—namely, that the reality in our everyday world is contingent. This recognition can be neither generalized nor translated into hypotheses that could be verified or disproven.

Perec's experimental process—"experimental" not in the strictly scientific sense—is relevant to design ethnography for the following reasons. First, it is *focused*, because Perec observes a very specific section of reality—Place Saint-Sulpice. Second, the process, which can seem paradoxical with regard to the first point, is *open*: Within the selected section, Perec observes more or less "everything." Of course, this openness does not necessarily lead him to see "more," much less to see "objectively": the latter could be achieved, for instance, by means of quantification. One might count the number of cars, pigeons, and people—but that is not the point. Perec simply sees something else—a blind spot that is hidden in everyday life. Third, his observation period is relatively *brief*: 3 days, which is not long in comparison to typical ethnographic studies, in which researchers spend months or even years immersed in other lifeworlds. The fact that a book was produced on the basis of 3 days in a café presupposes a large amount of notes. Thus, his observation is—fourth—*data intensive*. And fifth, finally, Perec *communicates* his observation. It is only possible for us to consider Perec and his experiment here because we have his text. Only this written form makes the inner world of his thought accessible to intersubjective connection. Without text, whatever Perec observed would remain a fluid event in his subjective consciousness—without the possibility of communicative connection.

Instead of asking what Perec sees, one might ask what he doesn't see: Perec no longer sees everyday reality in aggregate as an ensemble—or at least, he attempts to detach himself from it. *Ensemble* in this context means that when we see certain things and signs, we complete them to form a larger whole. We see a vehicle passing by quickly and know that it is a car. We do not see the car in its entirety—not every one of its four wheels, not the hood (much less what is under it), probably not the make of the car, and perhaps not even its color. We see (or hear) only a few individual elements and fill in the rest. The Polish immunologist and philosopher Ludwig Fleck describes this completion of the everyday as follows:

> We walk around without seeing any points, lines, angles, lights, or shadows, from which we would have to arrange 'what is this' by synthesis or reasoning, but we see at once a house, a memorial in square, a detachment of soldiers, a bookshop window, a group of children, a lady with a dog, all of them ready forms. (Fleck 1986, p. 134)

This completion takes place in our unconscious, but it comes about through knowledge that we have acquired and internalized in a process of socialization.

2.1 The Incorporation of Everyday Knowledge

The sociologists Hans-Georg Soeffner and Jürgen Raab write: "We do not perceive the world around us 'as such,' but rather, through seeing, we 'clip' it into shape for ourselves" (2004, p. 266). To illustrate this with an example from our everyday world of consumption: Shopping in a supermarket is a perfectly ordinary act for people in Western societies. If we shop frequently in the same supermarket, it becomes purely routine. We know what we are looking for and go automatically toward the right section. For instance, we want to buy a six-pack of beer, so we head for the appropriate area of the beverage section and look there for our favorite brand. We ignore the wine, just like we ignore the salad and the dairy products—unless we are tempted by clever marketing psychology to buy more than we originally wanted, but that is not at issue here. The point, rather, is that the routine act of "buying beer" delimits our perception and reduces complexity. Ultimately, we get our six-pack and bring it to the register. We pay in cash or with a credit card. We do not need to understand the monetarization of the economy or the credit system in order to complete the payment transaction. It suffices to have the money or a credit card.

As mundane as the experience of the supermarket is in everyday life, it is nonetheless a rather complex phenomenon dependent on a wealth of preconditions that already begins outside on the street with the signs (for instance, the logos), which indicate what is inside—that there, we will find food, beverages, household items, etc. It includes a very specific, often somewhat sterile, arrangement of the interior space and a taxonomic organization of products (all the different kinds of beer, for instance, in one place). It includes too a very specific material culture: shelving, registers, shopping carts, shopping baskets, products labeled with prices and bar codes and organized into specific categories. There are, roughly speaking, two types of people in a supermarket: employees and visitors. The first are identified by a particular uniform and by the fact that they are performing different activities in the supermarket than the visitors and are behaving differently. The second type includes customers, but also thieves and window-shoppers.

A supermarket depends on many preconditions: It could not exist without a capitalist market economy, industrial production, a monetarized economy, logistics, transportation, and advertising. A multitude of historical and cultural contingencies has led to the existence of supermarkets. We do not need to know this historical and cultural background in order to shop in a supermarket in everyday life. We use merely an implicit everyday knowledge—a *knowing-in-action* (Schön 1983, p. 51 ff.) or *skilled practices* (Ingold 2011, p. 60).

We come into the world more or less as a blank slate and develop our identity or habitus—by which is meant patterns of perception, classification, and interpretation of the world—though socialization (Bourdieu 2010, p. 257 ff.). We have internalized such knowledge and have no need to either reflect upon it or articulate it, since it resides in the self-evident features of everyday life (Soeffner 2004, p. 25). In the supermarket and in the *reality of everyday life* we operate to a certain extent "blindly." This *reality of everyday life* is only breached by a disruption. It is "interrupted by the appearance by a problem" (Berger and Luckmann 1967, p. 24). In the context of the supermarket, this happens for instance when the manned cash register is 1 day replaced by a self-service scanner. As long as both check-out systems exist in parallel, I can refuse the scanner—in the worst case, I will have to accept a longer wait for the register. But when the last register is closed, then I *must* learn to deal with the scanner despite my reluctance. The first interaction with the scanner forces me to reflect upon the routine nature of the act of shopping. Crises and disruptions can therefore lead us to reflect upon situations that we usually experience as "normal" (Schön 1983, p. 59 ff.).

One might now wonder what all this has to do with design. One initial answer is offered by the American Nobel Prize winner Herbert A. Simon. His thesis in his 1969 book, *The Science of the Artificial*, posited among other things that we live in an artificial—that is, man-made—world: We spend most of our time in spaces that have an artificially regulated temperature of around 20 °C and artificially pipe in or take away humidity. Even the impure air we inhale is something we produced ourselves (Simon 1996, p. 2).

Our world is artificial and designed. The longing for nature, so particularly widespread in the German-speaking world, is itself also something artificial—that is, a cultural construction that goes back to the reverential appreciation of nature in German Romanticism. And it does little or nothing to change the fact that we use smartphones, light switches, and refrigerators; that we wear clothes, get haircuts, take care of our bodies, ride bicycles, fly to other cities in airplanes, etc. That is to say, we are socialized into a designed world.

Socialization turns our reality into the *reality of everyday life*, which is the subject of the next chapter. This refers to the portion of reality that we experience as "normal"—which would include the Place Saint-Suplice in Paris, or any other place in the world that we walk through without giving it a second thought. We come from somewhere and are on our way to somewhere else. We *know* where we are. The place is simply there—we pay no attention to it.

References

Berger, P. L., & Luckmann, T. (1967). *The social construction of reality: A treatise in the sociology of knowledge*. New York: Anchor.

Bourdieu, P. (2010). *Distinction*. Oxon: Routledge.

Fleck, L. (1986). To look, to see, to know. In R. S. Cohen & T. Schnelle (Eds.), *Cognition and fact: Materials on Ludwik Fleck*. Dordrecht: Springer. https://doi.org/10.1007/978-94-009-4498-5.

Ingold, T. (2011). *Being alive: Essays on movement, knowledge and description*. New York: Routledge.

Maturana, H. R., & Varela, F. J. (2003). *El árbol del conocimiento. Las bases biológicas del entendimiento humano* [The tree of knowledge: The biological basis of human understanding]. Buenos Aires: Lumen.

Perec, G. (2010). *An attempt at exhausting a place in paris*. Cambridge, MA: Wakefield Press.

Schön, D. A. (1983). *The reflexive practitioner: How professionals think in action*. New York: Basic Books.

Simon, H. A. (1996). *The sciences of the artificial*. Cambridge, MA: MIT Press.

Soeffner, H. G. (2004). *Auslegung des Alltags—Der Alltag der Auslegung* [Interpretation of everyday life—The everyday life of interpretation]. Konstanz: UVK.

Soeffner, H. G., & Raab, J. (2004). Sehtechniken. Die Medialisierung des Sehens: Schnitt und Montage als Ästhetisierungsmittel medialer Kommunikation. [Techniques of seeing. The mediatisation of seeing: Editing and montage as means of the aesthetization of media communication]. In H. G. Soeffner (Ed.), *Auslegung des Alltags—Der Alltag der Auslegung* [Interpretation of everyday life—The everyday life of interpretation] (pp. 254–284). Konstanz: UVK.

Strauss, A. (2017). *Mirrors and masks: The search for identity*. New York: Routledge.

Open Access This chapter is licensed under the terms of the Creative Commons Attribution 4.0 International License (http://creativecommons.org/licenses/by/4.0/), which permits use, sharing, adaptation, distribution and reproduction in any medium or format, as long as you give appropriate credit to the original author(s) and the source, provide a link to the Creative Commons license and indicate if changes were made.

The images or other third party material in this chapter are included in the chapter's Creative Commons license, unless indicated otherwise in a credit line to the material. If material is not included in the chapter's Creative Commons license and your intended use is not permitted by statutory regulation or exceeds the permitted use, you will need to obtain permission directly from the copyright holder.

Chapter 3
The Everyday World and Intersubjectivity

Abstract We have learned through processes of socialization how to name and identify things, which helps us continually reduce complexity and bring order to the contingent world around us in our everyday life. At the same time, we move within many "small" social lifeworlds, or "multiple realities," that are disconnected from one another and each have a particular cultural grammar in which "things" are loaded with quite a variety of meanings that impact and alter our identities. Design ethnographers also move within these small social lifeworlds. They should neither judge these morally nor overwrite them with their own values, but rather meet them with openness and sensitivity.

Keywords Everyday world · Identity · Multiple realities · Language · Professional indifference

The concept of the *Lifeworld* was introduced into the philosophical discourse of phenomenology by Edmund Husserl. The background to this was the dominance of positivism, founded by August Comte in the nineteenth century (1908). Positivism required the sciences to exclude anything metaphysical and limit themselves only to what is verifiable. Physics came to be the dominant discipline and was regarded as a universal science. In his *Physique Sociale* (2010a, b), for instance, Adolphe Quetelet wanted to use physical methods to explain society. Husserl denounced this ethos of objectivity for lacking the experiential dimension: What people experience as *real* had, on his account, nothing to do with mathematical and physical formulas, but with our subjective being in the *lifeworld* (Husserl 1996, p. 54). Husserl's phenomenology was then developed further by existential philosophers such as Martin Heidegger and subsequently Jean-Paul Sartre and Merleau-Ponty. More interesting in the ethnographic context is Alfred Schütz's introduction of the concept of the *lifeworld* into sociology, where the *world of everyday life* is described as *paramount reality* (Schütz and Luckmann 1973, p. 3). *Paramount reality* is not to be understood ontologically. Rather, it is produced through stores of knowledge: from the way we tie our shoes to the operation of a light switch or the interface of a smartphone—we have internalized implicit knowledge. When we move around in our own city on public transport, we do so by rote. A ticket vending machine in Tokyo or a microbus ride on the outskirts of Mexico City, on the other hand, can pose an existential challenge. What we experience as "normal," then, has arisen out of the social context of our lifeworld. This social, intersubjective level is one side of the reality in which we live. The other is our individualized consciousness.

From a phenomenological point of view, consciousness is separate from the world (Husserl 1995, p. 66) and at once intertwined with it. Thus, it is not for instance possible for us to actually communicate our inner being through speech because all communication is based on a previously existing language. And language "typifies experience" (Berger and Luckmann 1967, p. 39).[1] The difficulty of communicating dreams demonstrates this: It is not possible to definitively translate a dream into the form of language (Berger and Luckmann 1967, p. 40). What should one describe? The moods and images that can only be conveyed through language to a limited extent? The actions, which are often diffuse? When we tell the events of a dream, this narrative is not a depiction of the dream but rather something produced through the act of the telling.

Language can also transcend the here and now: It can describe reality ("This is a tree") or negate it (the sentence "This is not a tree" can also be said of a tree).[2] In the language of religion, there are many terms that refer to the transcendent, which is at once absent and made accessible through naming the experience: "paradise," "hell," or "angel" are such terms. Phenomenology refers to this as *appresentation*, which is a kind of concomitant visualization of what is not there (Husserl 1995, p. 111; Schütz and Luckmann 1973, p. 11). In design theory, this term means that aesthetic phenomena evoke certain meanings and images: We see a house at night with a beer logo on it and hear music playing inside—so we know there is a bar in there without even looking inside. We even know what kind of bar it is: a hipster bar, a red-light bar, a jazz bar. We see individual signs and elements and complete the rest based on social knowledge.

There are "multiple realities" (Schütz 1945): the reality of quantum physics, art, religion, etc. But when we speak of the *world of everyday life*, we mean the segment of reality that we experience as "normal." A lecture hall is one example: It is designed in such a way that the attention of the majority of those present is directed to the front, where a professor gives a lecture. This hierarchy manifests itself in the seating arrangement, the tables, the projector, the screen, etc. A lecture hall obviously resembles a theatrical space, which makes it a "front region" (Goffman 1956, p. 67). The design of the lecture hall manifests, among other things, humanistic educational ideals and a politics that ascribes value to these ideals. A lecture hall elicits a specific behavior and social roles from the lecturers, the students, the janitorial staff, etc. A lecture hall is therefore a cultural construction. Construction

---

[1] Heidegger says that it is no longer the person who speaks, but language itself (1997, p. 143).

[2] Consider the well-known painting *La trahison des images* by René Magritte, which depicts a pipe and the sentence "Ceci n'est pas une pipe." The point is that this is not *actually* a pipe, but rather only an *image* of a pipe.

here does not mean something arbitrary, but rather something binding—or at least, it is the consequence of what was suggested by the Chicago sociologist William S. Thomas in his famous pronouncement: "If men define their situations as real, they are real in their consequences" (Thomas and Thomas 1928, p. 572).

One critique of the classical phenomenological theory of the lifeworld and everyday life is that the term is formulated in the singular, which suggests the above-mentioned notion of *Paramount Reality*, which is superior to other realities. The sociologist Benita Luckmann has remedied this deficit by pluralizing the concept of the lifeworld: On her account, modern man does not live in *one* lifeworld, but in *many* that cannot be hierarchized. Luckmann speaks of "small lifeworlds" that often have no relation to one another and exist only for a limited time (1978, p. 282 ff.). People thus operate in single-purpose-communities: A student, for example, operates in her parents' house, in her shared flat with her roommates, at a university, at a Kung Fu school, in a relationship, at a bar, where she works on weekends, etc. These "places" constitute specific social identities: She behaves differently at her parents' house, in her flat, and at the university. All these social "places" or situations are designed. They conceal a script and lead to specific role behavior. The description of these lifeworlds as *small* is not due to the number of people involved or the territorial size of the field, but to the fact that the complexity of possible redundancies is reduced to a certain system of relevance (Hitzler 2008, p. 136). These "places" can also be described as *sub-universes* (James 1921, p. 283 ff.) or *microcultures* (Cranz 2016, p. 40).

3.1 Symbolic Interaction and the Generalized Other

The fact that *small social lifeworlds* are experienced by individuals as "normal" is "a product of intersubjectivity, not of the individual" (Soeffner 2004, p. 22). The concept of intersubjectivity can be traced back to the pragmatism of George Herbert Mead. In his work, MIND, SELF & SOCIETY, Mead makes a distinction between a personal *I* and a social *Me* (2015, p. 173 ff.). The *I* is a spontaneous sensation, while *Me* is social patterns. Mead also distinguishes between *Play* and *Game* (2015, p. 152 ff.). In play, roles can be changed spontaneously in response to the situation, the way children do. In a *Game*, on the other hand, a *generalized other* is established, which may be demonstrated by the example of boxing. The only thing allowed in boxing is punches (straight, hook, and upwards hook) to the head and upper body—no low punches, no kicking, and no biting. Fighting takes place in an area delimited by a ring during a time delimited by acoustic signals, and not in the breaks in between. These rules are made binding by the *generalized other*. The boxer does not just expect his opponent to obey the rules, but he himself complies with them and incorporates them because his opponent, the trainers, referees, organizers, audience, sponsors, TV stations, boxing associations, etc., all expect it from him. If a boxer bites off his opponent's ear, then he substantially damages his identity as a boxer. The *generalized other* is thus something like an abstract and normative identity foil on which the boxer orients himself. This leads, on the one hand, to empathy—especially since one's own consciousness is simultaneously reflected in the *generalized other* and in the opponent. George Herbert Mead thus shows how human consciousness emerges; namely, on the basis of the reflection between a personal and a social identity. Similar approaches can be found in the thought of other representatives from the field of American Pragmatism—such as, for instance, Charles Horton Cooley, who called on sociologists to practice empathy toward people from other lifeworlds with his notion of "sympathetic introspection" (1909, p. 7) and who speaks of the "looking-glass-self" (1922, p. 184), in which the other becomes the mirror of the self.

On the basis of Mead's theory, Herbert Blumer developed symbolic interactionism—a micro-sociological theory relevant to design, which is founded on three premises (1986, p. 2):

1. Human beings act toward things on the basis of the meanings that the things have for them.
2. The meaning of such things is derived from, or arises out of, the social interaction that one has with one's fellows.
3. These meanings are handled in, and modified through, an interpretative process used by the person in dealing with the things they encounter.

With its anti-essentialist positions, symbolic interactionism often functions as a theoretical starting point for ethnographic field research (Prus 1996, 1997; Rock 2009). Harold Garfinkel advocates for a similar micro-sociological approach with his ethnomethodology, which also investigates how people constitute reality in their everyday worlds (Garfinkel 1967; Suchman et al. 2019). In conversational analysis (Sacks 1984), individual sequences of everyday communications are transcribed and analyzed in detail. This process aims to lay bare at the sociolinguistic level how everyday reality arises and becomes experienced as a certainty. In his now famous so-called *breaching experiments*, Garfinkel (1967, p. 35) challenged his students to behave in ways that differed from the norm—for instance, to act as guests in their own parents' home. In this way, deviant behavior is used to attempt to explore the limits of that which is considered *normal*. These disturbances of "natural" situations correspond to the interventions of design ethnography (Otto and Smith 2013, p. 11). Situations are "natural" when the researcher has not done anything to alter them (Dellwing and Prus 2012, p. 54 ff.). A design intervention, on the other hand, or a natural science experiment are "artificial" situations that have been evoked by the researcher.

Goffman observes everyday situations guided by the question: "What is it that's going on here?" (1986, p. 8). In this way, he seeks to find out how we ever got to the point where certain situations are experienced as normal to begin with. His assumption is that situations have certain frames that organize them in their existence as events. For instance, as is evident in how we handle physical proximity, we behave completely differently in different situations in which proximity arises. Western society has certain standards regarding what degrees of proximity are allowed in what situations, on which Goffman's studies on the territories of the self shed light.

At a Brazilian Jiu Jitsu school, we have very close physical contact with other people, with whom we otherwise have no contact at all outside that place. In an elevator, on the other hand, we might feel quite uncomfortable when it is crowded. An individual thus has certain *Territories of the Self* (Goffman 2010, p. 28 ff.): These are: (1) Personal Space, which is contiguous with the individual and can feel threatened in crowded elevators or vehicles. (2) The Stall, which is the visible and spatially delimited area that an individual has at their disposal, for instance on a bar stool or in a theater seat. (3) The Use Space, which is the space around the individual. (4) The Turn, which is a sequential position that an individual takes up in relation to others—for instance standing in line at a supermarket. (5) The Sheath, which is the skin that covers the body and the clothing that in turn covers the skin. (6) Professional Territory, which includes the objects that surround the body and are identified with the self—such easily portable possessions as jackets, hats, gloves, packs of cigarettes, matches, purses with their contents. (7) The Information Preserve, which is the store of information to which an individual would like to control access in the presence of others (this could be aspects of their biography as well as personal objects in pockets and purses). And (8) the Conversational Preserve, which means that an individual can decide with whom to enter into conversation.

These are informal rules that are culturally variable (Collier 1967, p. 39) and lack of compliance with them is understood as a violation of one's private sphere. This, however, depends on how the situation is framed. Thus, nakedness, for instance, can mean something different depending on the situational context—at the doctor, in public, in a sexual relationship, or in a life drawing class at an art studio. A naked model, according to Goffman, is in a certain sense not naked, but rather an "embodiment of the body" (1986, p. 78).

3.2 Professional Indifference and Lack of Moral Judgment

In the context of ethnography, we should turn to the aesthetic world with as unbiased a gaze as possible. Of course it is not possible to see the world from a neutral perspective, because there is no such thing as neutral and value-free knowledge. Nonetheless, Robert E. Park's premise—"A moral man cannot be a sociologist"— still applies (quoted in Girtler 2001, p. 82). Anyone who goes through the world in a moralizing and normative way is hardly likely to find out anything new about a lifeworld, but will at best confirm their own prejudices. This is clearly evident in the ethnographic research of the social anthropologist Sarah Pink on Spanish bullfighting (1997, 2013, p. 76 ff.). If she had either condemned or idealized bullfighting, then her point of view would have been one-sided and she would have found out very little about the cultural grammar in which bullfighting is embedded. Pink's impartiality is what allows her to open up different perspectives onto bullfighting.

This is why Crabtree et al. emphasize "professional indifference" (2012, p. 70 ff.) in design ethnography. Design ethnography aims to explore the grammar and patterns through which the reality of the lifeworlds it investigates is produced, not to colonize those worlds with their own values. It is especially important not to moralize when dealing with popular and everyday culture, such as online games, fast food, fashion, commerce, pornography, alcohol, selfies, and of course advertising. The value attached to these can be traced back to bourgeois educational ideals and the Frankfurt School, which distinguishes between a serious and a popular culture, whereby the former is "good" and the latter naturally "objectionable." This assessment is normative, which is not tenable from the perspective of cultural anthropology.

References

Berger, P. L., & Luckmann, T. (1967). *The social construction of reality: A treatise in the sociology of knowledge*. New York: Anchor.
Blumer, H. (1986). *Symbolic interaction: Perspective and method*. Berkeley: University of California Press.
Collier, J. (1967). *Visual anthropology: Photography as a research method*. New York: Holt, Rinehard and Winston.
Comte, A. (1908). *A general view of positivism*. London: George Routledge & Sons.
Cooley, C. H. (1909). *Social organization: A study of the larger mind*. New York: Shocken.
Cooley, C. H. (1922). *Human nature and the social order: A study of the larger mind*. New York: Shocken.
Crabtree, A., Roucefield, M., & Tolmie, P. (2012). *Doing design ethnography*. London: Springer.
Cranz, G. (2016). *Ethngraphy for designers*. New York: Routledge.
Dellwing, M., & Prus, R. (2012). *Einführung in die interaktionistische Ethnografie. Soziologie im Außendienst* [Introduction to interactionist ethnography: Sociology in the field]. Wiesbaden: Springer VS.
Garfinkel, H. (1967). *Studies in ethnomethodology*. Cambridge: Polity Press.
Girtler, R. (2001). *Methoden der Feldforschung* [Field research methods]. Cologne: Böhlau.
Goffman, E. (1956). *The presentation of self in everyday life*. Edinburgh: University of Edinburgh.
Goffman, E. (1986). *Frame analysis: An essay on the organization of experience*. Boston: Northeastern University Press.
Goffman, E. (2010). *Relations in public: Microstudies of the public order*. New Brunswick: Transaction.
Heidegger, M. (1997). *Gesamtausgabe. 1. Abteilung: Veröffentlichte Schriften 1910-1976, Band 10: Der Satz vom Grund*. Frankfurt a. M.: Vittorio Klostermann.
Hitzler, R. (2008). Lebenswelt und Erlebniswelten [Lifeworld and worlds of experience]. In J. Raab, M. Pfadenhauer, P. Stegmaier, J. Dreher, & B. Schnettler (Eds.), *Phänomenologie und Soziologie. Theoretische Positionen, aktuelle Problemfelder und empirische Umsetzungen* [Phenomenology and sociology: Theoretical positions, current problem areas and empirical implementations] (pp. 131–140). Wiesbaden: Springer VS.
Husserl, E. (1995). *Cartesianische Meditationen* [Cartesian meditations]. Hamburg: Felix Meiner.
Husserl, E. (1996). *Die Krisis der europäischen Wissenschaften und die transzendentale Phänomenologie* [The European science crisis and transcendental phenomenology]. Hamburg: Felix Meiner.
James, W. (1921). *The principles of psychology*. New York: Dover.
Luckmann, B. (1978). The small life-worlds of modern man. In T. Luckmann (Ed.), *Phenomenology and sociology* (pp. 275–290). New York: Penguin Books.
Mead, G. H. (2015). *Mind, self & society*. Chicago: University of Chicago Press.

References

Otto, T., & Smith, R. C. (2013). Design anthropology: A distinct style of knowing. In W. Gunn, T. Otto, & R. C. Smith (Eds.), *Design anthropology: Theory and practice* (pp. 1–29). London: Bloomsbury.

Pink, S. (1997). *Women and bullfighting: Gender, sex and the consumption of tradition.* London: Bloomsbury Academic.

Pink, S. (2013). *Doing visual ethnography.* London: Sage.

Prus, R. (1996). *Symbolic interaction and ethnographic research: Intersubjectivity and the study of human lives experience.* Albany, NY: State University of New York Press.

Prus, R. (1997). *Subcultural mosaic and intersubjective realities: An ethnographic research agenda for pragmatizing the social sciences.* Albany, NY: State University of New York Press.

Quetelet, A. (2010a). *Sur l'homme et le développement de ses facultés, ou Essai de physique sociale, Tome 1* [On man and the development of his faculties, or essay on social physics, Vol. 1]. Charleston, SC: Book Surge.

Quetelet, A. (2010b). *Sur l'homme et le développement de ses facultés, ou essai de physique sociale, Tome 2* [On man and the development of his faculties, or essay on social physics, Vol. 2]. Charleston, SC: Book Surge.

Rock, P. (2009). Symbolic interactionism and ethnography. In P. Atkinson, A. Coffey, S. Delamont, J. Lofland, & L. Lofland (Eds.), *Handbook of ethnography* (pp. 26–38). London: Sage.

Sacks, H. (1984). On doing 'being ordinary'. In J. Atkinson & J. Heritage (Eds.), *Structures of social action: Studies in conversational analysis* (pp. 413–440). Cambridge: Cambridge University Press.

Schütz, A. (1945). On multiple realities. *Philosophy and Phenomenological Research, 5*(4), 533–576.

Schütz, A., & Luckmann, T. (1973). *The structures of the life-world.* Evanston, IL: Northwestern University Press.

Soeffner, H. G. (2004). *Auslegung des Alltags—Der Alltag der Auslegung* [Interpretation of everyday life—The everyday life of interpretation]. Konstanz: UVK.

Suchman, L., Gerst, D., & Krämer, H. (2019). "If you want to understand the big issues, you need to understand the everyday practices that constitute them." Lucy Suchman in conversation with Dominik Gerst & Hannes Krämer. *FQS Forum Qualitative Social Research, 20*(2). Retrieved August 17, 2019, from http://www.qualitative-research.net/index.php/fqs/article/view/3252/4386

Thomas, W. I., & Thomas, D. S. (1928). *The child in America: Behavior problems and programs.* New York: Knopf.

Open Access This chapter is licensed under the terms of the Creative Commons Attribution 4.0 International License (http://creativecommons.org/licenses/by/4.0/), which permits use, sharing, adaptation, distribution and reproduction in any medium or format, as long as you give appropriate credit to the original author(s) and the source, provide a link to the Creative Commons license and indicate if changes were made.

The images or other third party material in this chapter are included in the chapter's Creative Commons license, unless indicated otherwise in a credit line to the material. If material is not included in the chapter's Creative Commons license and your intended use is not permitted by statutory regulation or exceeds the permitted use, you will need to obtain permission directly from the copyright holder.

Chapter 4
Design Research: Immersion and Intervention

Abstract Research is part of any design praxis. But there is no consensus about how exactly research should be conducted. This is in part due to the fact that the disciplines of design have varied historically and are today greatly differentiated from one another. This chapter sketches out how design ethnography does research: it does not test previously constructed hypotheses, but rather explores and leads into new territories, which makes it risky and adventurous. It concerns itself with singularities, which means it does not necessarily need to generalize its findings. It can break with convention, push boundaries, and expand conceptual horizons. It is abductive, constructivist, and reflexive. It develops hypotheses that can be transferred into design.

Keywords Abduction · Design discipline · Research through design · Risk · Serendipity

Designers primarily create something new. They see reality—and in it the potential for change (Fulton Suri 2011, p. 31). But a design process never starts from scratch, because "to design is always to *redesign*. There is always something that exists first as a given, as an issue, as a problem" (Latour 2008, p. 5). Design makes reference to something preexisting from which it must differentiate itself. Design requires and generates knowledge.

Generally, the concept of design is associated with industrialization and the division of labor. These are the processes that led to the decoupling of conception and production. Products are designed first and then mass-produced afterward. Industrially produced things are "made more beautiful" and "given a form." In the German-speaking world, until the 1970s designers were referred to as "form-givers" (Krippendorff 2013, p. 29). Design-specific functionalism should be mentioned in this context. In 1896, the architect Louis H. Sullivan, of the architectural (not to be confused with the sociological) Chicago School, formulated the famous dictum "*form ever follows function*" (1896, p. 408). The form thus aesthetisizes the intended use, as illustrated in an exemplary manner by an aerodynamic car. Functionalism was taken further by the Bauhaus, where the focus was on eschewing all ornament and flourish and practicality stood at the center (Gropius 1996, p. 149 ff.). Klaus Krippendorff criticizes functionalism as "an expression of blind acceptance of the role assigned to designers by society, and especially by their industrial clients" (2013, p. 28). Krippendorff pleads instead for a semantic shift: *"People can neither see nor react to the physical properties of things. They always act in accordance with what the things mean to them"* (2013, p. 75).

Other theorists have also criticized the notion of design as "form-giving." In the 1970s, Bazon Brock called for a "socio-design" and an "expansion of the concept of design" that would emancipate itself from the industrial production of goods to focus on the formation of ways of life, values, and linguistic gestures (1977, p. 446). With this idea of socio-design, Brock formulated something that is inherent in design itself: Design is something genuinely social, which is why Brandes et al. speak of the "sociality of design" (2009, p. 90 ff.). The cultural sociologist Yana Milev criticizes the fact that "the utilitarian and doggedly functional view of design" ideologizes design as a progressive force for consumer goods (2011, p. 46). She calls for "an anthropological and participatory form of design research" (Milev 2011, p. 46).

Undoubtedly, the concept of design has been undergoing an explosive expansion for some time now, which is reflected in the proliferation of differentiated disciplines such as game design, interaction design, experience design, event design, fashion design, graphic design, communication design, system design, spatial design, cultural design, knowledge visualization, etc. Design has thus emancipated itself from thingness and form-giving. According to the design theorist Claudia Mareis, the concept of design encompasses "an immense spectrum of discourses, methods, activities, and artifacts, from the design of mass-produced goods to individually formed unique objects to generalized planning and problem-solving processes" (2014, p. 37).

This "cultural technique of 'designing'" (Mareis 2014, p. 152 ff.) is therefore situated between different disciplines—which is precisely why perspectives within design can be ascribed to distinct individual disciplines. A design problem may be defined as social, economic, ecological, political, formal, ergonomic, technical, or atmospheric—whereby these definitions already say something about the direction in which the solutions will be sought (Götz 2010, p. 55 f.).

The sociologist Franz Schultheis argues for a disciplining of design so that it can "transform itself [...] from an 'illegitimate art' into a legitimate field of scientific theory and research" (2005, p. 68). Anthropologist Lucy A. Suchman calls for design to find its "place"—"to locate itself as a one (albeit multiple) figure and practice of change" (2011, p. 3). The fact that theory and practice play a part in design does not make this search for location any easier. Although design is fundamentally practical, it is not free of theory. This is evident from scholarly journals such as *Design Studies* and *Design Issues*, the *Deutsche Gesellschaft für Designtheorie und -forschung* (www.dgtf.de) and die English *Design Research Society*. Mareis speaks of *Design as Knowledge Culture* (2011) and traces the interpositioning of the discourses of design and knowledge since the emergence of the *Design Methods Movement* in the 1960 (Gregory 1966; Mareis 2010, p. 17 ff., 2011, p. 34 ff., 2014, p. 162 ff.). Sydney A. Gregory defines *Design Science* as a discipline that deals with the study, investigation, and accumulation of knowledge in design processes and their essential operations (1966, p. 323). In his book *Designerly Ways of Knowing,* design theorist Nigel Cross proposes the thesis that individual figures such as Le Courbusier had already laid the foundation for the Design Methods Movement of the 1960s back in the 1920s (2007a, p. 119 ff.). Cross distinguishes between three categories of design research (2007b, p. 48): (1) *Design epistemology—study of designerly ways of knowing*; (2) *Design praxeology—study of the practices and processes of design;* and (3) *Design phenomenology—study of the form and configuration of artifacts.*

4.1 Warm, Involving, and Risky

Bruno Latour writes: "Science is certainty; research is uncertainty. Science is supposed to be cold, straight, and detached; research is warm, involving, and risky" (1998, p. 208). Research leads into unknown territory. The knowledge it generates is particular and based on experience, not universal. This is especially the case for ethnography: "Ethnographic truths are thus inherently *partial*—committed and incomplete" (Clifford 1986, p. 7).

In contrast to *Science* the term *Research* implies that previously existing knowledge functions as a reference point, given that something is being searched for *again*. This knowledge can be explicit or implicit. We have recourse to explicit knowledge if it has already been articulated—for instance, when we access cultural studies texts in libraries, or search on-line databases for e-papers. Implicit knowledge signifies internalized practical knowledge—it is the everyday knowledge discussed above, which we use among other things to move about in the supermarket. Uriel Orlow writes:

> At stake, then, is not chiefly a form of new knowledge that is teleologically targeted, but rather a reticulated, branched feeling out of latent knowledge that is in part already there, but is not immediately visible or graspable, and which is made accessible again and combined anew in the process of research. (Orlow 2014, p. 201)

This aligns with the thesis that people know more than they can articulate (Schön 1983, p. 51 ff.). By observing, articulating, and translating into text practical and everyday knowledge, we make it explicit—and make it possible to reflect on it. In her various studies, Sarah Pink, for example, has ethnographically investigated how long-standing everyday practices—such as those in the kitchen (2012, p. 48ff.), the laundry (2012, p. 66 ff.), or the garden (2012, p. 84 ff.)—are carried out and what specific knowledge the relevant actors possess.

Design ethnography has many possibilities to experiment with methods. It can intervene, disrupt situations, develop and test prototypes. It does not have to adhere to a linear research process, but rather involves iterative processes and increased awareness. Designers should operate with reflective practices (Schön 1983) and quickly switch between the roles of researcher and designer. In research, they attempt to shed light on the things and connections of our social and cultural world from as many perspectives as possible. This requires openness, empathy, sensitivity, exploration, and participatory approaches undertaken with the people in the field of inquiry. In design, on the other hand, they adopt an attitude that focuses as much as possible on a small, identifiable, and changeable portion of reality—that is to say, a "place" where design can have an impact and change something. Design always pertains to something that does not yet exist and is therefore speculative—in contrast to descriptive ethnography in social research. Design wants to change the world. Every change is driven by assumptions that are prospective. Design is always directed towards an (uncertain) future and helps shape it: "Everyone designs who devises courses of action aimed at changing existing situations into preferred ones" (Simon 1996, p. 111). In a design ethnography, these two dimensions—the descriptive and the prospective—come together. These are "Ethnographies of the Possible" (Halse 2013), which do not simply investigate social lifeworlds but also ask: "What happens if we look at it this way?" (Halse 2013, p. 182). Design thinks in alternatives. Design is speculative. Speculation requires avoiding prejudices and moral judgments and striving for an unbiased view. Design proceeds from empirical observations and hypotheses that change people's behavior, interactions, and even identities. Design holds a conception of mankind that to a certain extent it itself brings forth.

4.2 Research Through Design

There is a typology occasionally called upon in the context of design research that originally goes back to the art theorist Herbert Read (1944) and was adapted for art and design by Christopher Frayling: *research into art and design*, *research through art and design* and *research for art and design* (Frayling 1993, p. 5). Alain Findeli has modified this typology specifically for design, replacing the focus on art history with a present-oriented orientation on popular culture (2004, p. 42). He proposes the following three types of design research (2004, p. 41 ff.):

- *Research for design*: These are projects at design schools in which students do research before designing a product or system. It is also applied in professional design practice—for instance, in the research departments of design firms. This research often draws on existing knowledge.
- *Research on design*: This category is mainly practiced at colleges and universities. Here design is put in the context of academic theory (economics, art history, technology, sociology, etc.).
- *Research through design:* This research centers on people and is active. Design here operates as a method to generate knowledge. It requires praxis, exploration, and self-reflection.

Findeli criticizes the first two approaches. *Research for design* has no memory. It begins anew with every project and because for the most part it draws on already existing knowledge, it is not accepted in the sciences. The converse is the case for *research on design*, which may have a place in scholarly discourse, but has no relevance for design praxis. Findeli favors *research through design*, which he describes as "project-led research" (2004, p. 44). He emphasizes the potential of interpretive (hermeneutics, phenomenology, personal history) and active methods (participatory research, action research, grounded theory, etc.) (2004, p. 45).

Design ethnography corresponds to what Findeli calls "project-led research." It is interpretative, qualitative, engaged, active, constructivistic, interactionistic, phenomenological, explorative, and abductive. It is—to use Bruno Latour's differentiation between research and science—a *risky* research method. It can disrupt conventions, push boundaries, and expand mental horizons. Design ethnography can mean passively observing social situations in order to alter them afterward through intervention, and then observe them again, etc. It is not a linear but an iterative process, in which observation, analysis, and conception are inextricable:

> Design ethnography offers a powerful way to examine the circulations of meanings, objects, and identities in diffuse time-space and bring these to fruition, not in new description of localities, but in new objects and services that will make sense to these localities. (Salvador et al. 1999, p. 41)

The design ethnographer observes actions—and acts. They generate knowledge—through praxis. Design ethnography not only investigates designed realities—it also brings them forth.

This explorative approach eludes inductive and deductive methods. Proceeding inductively leads to generalizing one's own observations—even though these may have no universal relevance at all but are only specific to the case. If I observe white swans on the lake shore, this does not mean that many swans are white (Popper 1935, p. 1). The hypothesis that all swans are white is therefore only valid until a gray swan comes along; then it is falsified (Popper 1935, p. 5 ff.). Those who proceed deductively from the start of their research project will construct and test their hypotheses. This begs the questions, however—where did the preliminary knowledge for the construction come from, given that there is still very little knowledge available about the research field at the start of the investigation. Much of what we know comes from self-referential peer-group discourses, digital bubbles, and mass media. It would be banal to "test" this pre-given knowledge in the context of a social lifeworld. Anyone who knows from the start what they are looking for will view reality through tunnel vision and will therefore fail to see many phenomena that might turn out to be relevant (Blumer 1986, p. 21 ff.). Hypotheses constructed in advance carry the risk of narrowing one's perspective in the field. At best, hypotheses should be understood as tools that lead one into the field but become obsolete there through serendipity:

> If a man sets out on an expedition, determined to prove certain hypotheses, if he is incapable of changing his views constantly and casting them off ungrudgingly under the pressure of evidence, needless to say his work will be worthless. (Malinowski 1932, p. 16)

4.3 Contingency and Serendipity

The founders of Grounded Theory described their methods as inductive (Glaser and Strauss 1995, p. 114). Strübing describes this as an "inductivist self-misunderstanding" and assigns Grounded Theory to abduction (2008, p. 44 ff.). Abduction, which was introduced into the social sciences by Charles S. Pierce (2004, p. 209 ff.), is intended to lead to new insights specifically through experience, *not* through paths charted by logic. In the context of abduction, Jo Reichertz puts emphasis on the new, which flares up as an idea: "[...] abduction is sensible and scientific as a form of inference, however it reaches to the sphere of deep insight and new knowledge" (2007, p. 216). The phenomenologist Thomas S. Eberle sees abduction as an attitude that consists in curiosity, intense observation, and the openness to bracket one's own convictions (2011, p. 41). The design theorist Michael Erlhoff points to the potential of fuzziness and undogmatic approaches in the context of design research (2010, p. 41). The sociologist Anne Honer insists that an ethnographer must always be ready to allow themselves to become confused, experience shocks, and set aside their moral judgments for a time (2008, p. 203).

An abductive process entails a kind of chaotic interplay of induction and deduction, in which observations and internalized implicit practical knowledge (of participants in a field) are continually made explicit. It is an immersive process in which one becomes sensitized to a lifeworld to the point that one discovers something about its "cosmology" (Goffman 1986, p. 27). The point is that the researcher does not simply find something in the data, but also *adds* something to it, which makes abduction constructivist (Bryant and Charmaz 2007, p. 44 ff.). With abduction, new hypotheses can be developed that could be transferred into the process of design.

Methods therefore must not be applied dogmatically—rather, they may and should be adapted and developed further. Ton Otto and Rachel Charlotte Smith emphasize the potential for interventions in and disruptions of natural situations in the context of design ethnography (2013, p. 12). To prevent the research from becoming completely arbitrary, these methods must be made transparent, that is to say, they should be reflected upon. Only then can the demand for intersubjectivity in research be satisfied. In this respect, design research resembles a voyage of discovery—but one that is very well documented, charted, and reflected upon, so it is always comprehensible to those who were not a part of it.

In the context of abduction, it is important to consider serendipity. Serendipity refers to what Ludwig Fleck described as the "Columbus Effect" (1980, p. 91): Columbus was looking for a new route to India and discovered America. The history of science can point to many such examples: for instance, penicillin, LSD, or Viagra. It is in the nature of searching that one enters into new territory. "The fundamental problem of such a process of searching consists in the fact that it is not possible to precisely determine what one doesn't know" (Rheinberger 2014, p. 232). For this reason, Peter Friedrich Stephan suggests that not knowing should no longer be seen exclusively as a deficit, but rather also as a resource (2010, p. 85). Michael Dellwing and Robert Prus posit the thesis that very open, interactionist ethnography is *per se* serendipitous. At the same time, however—as the examples from the history of science demonstrate—the pure natural sciences are not free of it either, although they are not allowed to show it, since they do not ascribe any meaningful role to chaos and contingency (Dellwing and Prus 2012, p. 206). Thus, what is hidden in the pure sciences may be revealed in design ethnography. Dealing with serendipity requires openness, attentiveness, and sensitivity.

References

Blumer, H. (1986). *Symbolic interaction: Perspective and method*. Berkeley: University of California Press.
Brandes, U., Erlhoff, M., & Schemmann, N. (2009). *Designtheorie und Designforschung* [Design theory and design research]. Paderborn: Fink.
Brock, B. (1977). Objektwelt und die Möglichkeit des subjektiven Lebens—Begriff und Konzept des Sozio-Designs [The object world and the possibility of subjective life: Terms and concepts of socio-design]. In B. Brock (Ed.), *Ästhetik als Vermittlung. Autobiografie eines Generalisten* [Aesthetics as mediation: Autobiography of a generalist] (pp. 446–449). Cologne: Dumont.
Bryant, A., & Charmaz, K. (2007). Grounded theory in historical perspective: An epistemological account. In A. Bryant & K. Charmaz (Eds.), *Handbook of grounded theory* (pp. 31–57). London: Sage.
Clifford, J. (1986). Introduction: Partial truths. In J. Clifford & G. E. Marcus (Eds.), *Writing culture: The poetics and politics of ethnography* (pp. 1–26). Los Angeles: University of California Press.
Cross, N. (2007a). *Designerly ways of knowing*. Basel: Birkhäuser.
Cross, N. (2007b). From a design science to a design discipline: Understanding designerly ways of knowing and thinking. In R. Michel (Ed.), *Design research now* (pp. 41–54). Basel: Birkhauser.
Dellwing, M., & Prus, R. (2012). *Einführung in die interaktionistische Ethnografie. Soziologie im Außendienst* [Introduction to interactionist ethnography: Sociology in the field]. Wiesbaden: Springer VS.
Eberle, T. S. (2011). Abduktion in phänomenologischer Perspektive [Abduction in a phenomenological perspective]. In N. Schröer & O. Bidlo (Eds.), *Die Entdeckung des Neuen. Qualitative Sozialforschung als Hermeneutische Wissenssoziologie* [The discovery of the new: Qualitative social research as a hermeneutical sociology of knowledge] (pp. 21–44). Wiesbaden: Springer VS.
Erlhoff, M. (2010). Aspekte der Designwissenschaft [Aspects of design science]. In F. Romero-Tejedor & W. Jonas (Eds.), *Positionen zur Designwissenschaft* [Positions on design science] (pp. 37–41). Kassel: University Press.
Findeli, A. (2004). Die projektgeleitete Forschung. Eine Methode der Designforschung [Project-led research: A method of design research]. Swiss Design Network Symposium. HGK Basel, pp. 41–51. Retrieved May 11, 2017, from http://swissdesignnetwork.ch/src/publication/erstesdesignforschungssymposium-2004/ErstesDesignForschungssymposium_2004.pdf
Fleck, L. (1980). *Entstehung und Entwicklung einer wissenschaftlichen Tatsache: Einführung in die Lehre vom Denkstil und Denkkollektiv* [Origin and development of a scientific fact: Introduction to the theory of thinking style and the collective of ideas]. Berlin: Suhrkamp.
Frayling, C. (1993). Research in art and design. *Royal College of Art Research Paper, 1*(1), 1–5.
Fulton Suri, J. (2011). Poetic observation: What designers make of what they see. In A. J. Clarke (Ed.), *Design anthropology: Object culture in the 21st century* (pp. 16–32). New York: Springer.

Glaser, B. G., & Strauss, A. L. (1995). *Discovering grounded theory: Strategies for qualitative research*. New Brunswick: Transaction.
Goffman, E. (1986). *Frame analysis: An essay on the organization of experience*. Boston: Northeastern University Press.
Götz, M. (2010). Design als Abenteuer [Design as adventure]. In F. Romero-Tejedor & W. Jonas (Eds.), *Positionen zur Designwissenschaft* [Positions in design science] (pp. 53–57). Kassel: University Press.
Gregory, S. A. (1966). *The design method*. London: Butterworth.
Gropius, W. (1996). Grundsätze der Bauhausproduktion [Principles of Bauhaus production]. In A. Preiss & K. J. Winkler (Eds.), *Weimarer Konzepte. Die Kunst- und Bauhochschule 1860–1995* [Weimar concepts: The Art and Architecture School 1860–1995] (pp. 149–151). Weimar: Verlag und Datenbank für Geisteswissenschaften (VDG).
Halse, J. (2013). Ethnographies of the possible. In W. Gunn, T. Otto, & R. C. Smith (Eds.), *Design anthropology: Theory and practice* (pp. 180–196). London: Bloomsbury.
Honer, A. (2008). Lebensweltanalyse in der Ethnografie [Life world analysis in ethnography]. In U. Flick, E. von Kardorff, & I. Steinke (Eds.), *Qualitative Forschung. Ein Handbuch* [Qualitative research: A manual] (pp. 194–204). Reinbek: Rowohlt.
Krippendorff, K. (2013). *Die semantische Wende. Eine neue Grundlage fürs Design* [The semantic turn: A new foundation for design]. Basel: Birkhäuser.
Latour, B. (1998). From the world of science to the world of research? *Science, 280*, 208–209.
Latour, B. (2008). A cautious Prometheus? A few steps toward a philosophy of design (with special attention to Peter Sloterdijk). *Proceedings of the 2008 annual International Conference of the Design History Society—Falmouth, 3–6 September 2009*. Retrieved July 15, 2019, from http://www.bruno-latour.fr/sites/default/files/112-DESIGN-CORNWALL-GB.pdf
Malinowski, B. (1932). *Argonauts of the Western Pacific*. London: George Routledge & Sons.
Mareis, C. (2010). Entwerfen—Wissen—Produzieren. Designforschung im Anwendungskontext [Design—Knowledge—Production: Design research in an application context]. In C. Mareis, G. Joost, & K. Kimpel (Eds.), *Entwer-fen—Wissen—Produzieren. Designforschung im Anwendungskontext* [Design—Knowledge—Production: Design research in an application context] (pp. 9–32). Bielefeld: Transcript.
Mareis, C. (2011). *Design als Wissenskultur. Interferenzen zwischen Design- und Wissensdiskursen seit 1960* [Design as a culture of knowledge: Interferences between design and knowledge discourses since 1960]. Bielefeld: Transcript.
Mareis, C. (2014). *Theorien des Designs. Zur Einführung* [Theories of design: An introduction]. Hamburg: Junius.
Milev, Y. (2011). *Emergency Design. Anthropotechniken des Über/Lebens* [Emergency design: Anthropotechnics of survival]. Berlin: Merve.
Orlow, U. (2014). Recherchieren [Doing research]. In J. Badura, S. Dubach, A. Haarmann, D. Mersch, A. Rey, C. Schenker, & G. T. Pérez (Eds.), *Künstlerische Forschung. Ein Handbuch* [Artistic research: A handbook] (pp. 201–204). Zurich: Diaphanes.
Otto, T., & Smith, R. C. (2013). Design anthropology: A distinct style of knowing. In W. Gunn, T. Otto, & R. C. Smith (Eds.), *Design anthropology: Theory and practice* (pp. 1–29). London: Bloomsbury.
Pierce, C. S. (2004). Aus den Pragmatismus-Vorlesungen [From the pragmatism lectures]. In J. Strübing & B. Schnettler (Eds.), *Methodologie interpretativer Sozialforschung* [Methodology of interpretative social research] (pp. 203–222). Konstanz: Klassische Grundlagentexte, UVK.
Pink, S. (2012). *Situating everyday life*. London: Sage.
Popper, K. (1935). Logik der Forschung. Zur Erkenntnistheorie der modernen Naturwissenschaft [Logic of research: On the epistemology of modern science]. In P. Frank & M. Schlick (Eds.), *Schriften zur wissenschaftlichen Weltauffassung, Band 9* [Writings on the scientific worldview, Vol. 9]. Vienna: Springer.
Read, H. (1944). *Education through art*. London: Faber and Faber.

References

Reichertz, J. (2007). Abduction: The logic of discovery in grounded theory. In A. Bryant & K. Charmaz (Eds.), *The SAGE handbook of grounded theory* (pp. 214–228). London: Sage.

Rheinberger, H. J. (2014). Über Serendipität—Forschen und finden [On serendipity—Researching and finding]. In G. Boehm, E. Alloa, O. Budelacci, & G. Wildgruber (Eds.), *Imagination. Suchen und finden* [Imagination: Searching and finding] (pp. 232–243). Paderborn: Fink.

Salvador, T., Bell, G., & Anderson, K. (1999). Design ethnography. *Design Management Journal, 10*(4), 35–41. https://doi.org/10.1111/j.1948-7169.1999.tb00274.x.

Schön, D. A. (1983). *The reflexive practitioner: How professionals think in action*. New York: Basic Books.

Schultheis, F. (2005). Disziplinierung des Designs [Disciplining of design]. *Forschungslandschaften im Umfeld des Designs* [Research landscapes in the design setting] (pp. 65–84). Zurich: Swiss Design Network.

Simon, H. A. (1996). *The sciences of the artificial*. Cambridge, MA: MIT Press.

Stephan, P. F. (2010). Wissen und Nicht-Wissen im Entwurf [Knowing and not knowing in design]. In C. Mareis, G. Joost & K. Kimpel (Eds.), *Entwerfen—Wissen—Produzieren. Designforschung im Anwendungskontext* [Design—Knowledge—Production: Design research in an application context] (pp. 81–99). Bielefeld: Transcript.

Strübing, J. (2008). *Grounded Theory. Zur sozialtheoretischen und epistemologischen Fundierung des Verfahrens und der empirisch begründeten Theoriebildung* [Grounded theory: Toward a socio-theoretical and epistemological foundation of process and the development of empirically founded theory]. Wiesbaden: Springer VS.

Suchman, L. A. (2011). Anthropological relocations and the limits of design. *Annual Review Anthropology, 40*, 1–18. https://doi.org/10.1146/annurev.anthro.041608.105640.

Sullivan, L. H. (1896, March). The tall office building artistically considered. *Lippincot's Magazine*, pp. 403–409.

Open Access This chapter is licensed under the terms of the Creative Commons Attribution 4.0 International License (http://creativecommons.org/licenses/by/4.0/), which permits use, sharing, adaptation, distribution and reproduction in any medium or format, as long as you give appropriate credit to the original author(s) and the source, provide a link to the Creative Commons license and indicate if changes were made.

The images or other third party material in this chapter are included in the chapter's Creative Commons license, unless indicated otherwise in a credit line to the material. If material is not included in the chapter's Creative Commons license and your intended use is not permitted by statutory regulation or exceeds the permitted use, you will need to obtain permission directly from the copyright holder.

Chapter 5
Methods and Aspects of Field Research

Abstract This chapter lays out the history of ethnography, which began with travel narratives in antiquity and came to be used as a method in anthropology and urban sociology in the early twentieth century. Discussed, among other things, are the researcher's role in the field and ethical considerations, as well as methods such as observation, interviews, digital, visual, and participatory ethnography, and the question of the documentation of design ethnography research. These are dealt with here within the specific context of design ethnography, which is usually significantly shorter in duration than the typical ethnographies in anthropology and cultural sociology and may seek not only to investigate a situation but also potentially to alter it.

Keywords Participatory action research · Defamiliarization · Digital ethnography · Ethnographic interview · Ethnographic observation · Visual research

The term *ethnography* can be traced back to the ancient Greek *éthnos* (foreign people) and *graphé* (writing). A description of a foreign society presupposes two things: First, people who are engaged in ethnography must be mobile in order to have come into contact with foreign societies to begin with. Second, they require media such as writing, drawing, images, etc., in order to record their observations. The oldest ethnographies are travelogues, some of which had already been composed in ancient Greece: The geographer Skylax, the merchant Pytheas von Massalia, and the historian Herodotus reported on their journeys to the Near East. In the fourteenth century, the Muslim scholar Ibn Battûta wrote about his travels to Mekka, India, and China. Marco Polo's reports of his travels in China—the authenticity of which, by the way, was doubted at the time because there were too few marvelous creatures described in them—are of course well known. Equally disputed was the travelogue of the German adventurer Hand Staden, who journeyed to Brazil in the sixteenth century with Portuguese conquerors and was supposedly held captive there by cannibals.

Later, ethnographic reports were written by missionaries, who explored indigenous societies in order to Christianize them. It was not until the nineteenth century that such investigations would be liberated from missionary ambitions, thus clearing a path for actual anthropological research. In the late nineteenth century, ethnography became a sociological and anthropological method. The American anthropologist Frank Hamilton Cushing, who spent many years during the 1880s with the indigenous Zuni tribes in New Mexico, was one of the first to write ethnographic reports in the social scientific sense (1988). The actual foundation of the method as such is ascribed to the Polish anthropologist Bronislaw Malinowski, who conducted long-term field work on the Trobriand Islands in Papua New Guinea in the 1910s (1932).

5.1 The Foreign Worlds Next Door and Defamiliarization

The ethnographic method was also developed around the same time, in the early twentieth century, by the Chicago School of sociology—although here the encounter with the foreign took place not on the far-off Trobriand Islands but just next door (Deegan 2009, pp. 11–25, 119–164). Robert E. Park, on of the founders of the Chicago School, said to his students:

> You have been told to go grubbing in the library, thereby accumulating a mass of notes and liberal coating of grime. You have been told to choose problems wherever you can find musty stacks of routine records based on trivial schedules prepared by tired bureaucrats and filled out by reluctant applicants for aid or fussy do-gooders or indifferent clerks. This is called "getting your hands dirty in real social research." Those who counsel you are wise and honorable; the reasons they offer are of great value. But one more thing is needful; first hand observation. Go and sit in the lounges of luxury hotels and on the doorsteps of the flophouses; sit on the Gold Coast settees and the slum shakedowns; sit in the orchestra hall and in the Star and Garter burlesque. In short, gentlemen, go to get the seat of your pants dirty in real social research. (Park, cited in Prus 1996, p. 119)

It is not by chance that Park calls on his students to go out to the luxury hotels and to the emergency shelters in the slums. In the late nineteenth century, migration led to a great degree of urbanization and pluralization of society, particularly in the northeast of the USA, but also in other major centers. Cities like Chicago and New York developed into gigantic metropolises in the span of a few decades. But it was not only the quantitative dimension of these urbanization processes that was new. The influx of immigrants also altered society qualitatively. It undermined the cultural dominance of the WASP (White Anglo-Saxon Protestant) in the northeast. The predominantly Protestant society was now confronted with Jews from Ukraine, Catholics from Ireland and Italy, and Germans, who were thought to be beer-guzzling atheists. To this day, the China Towns and Little Italies in Chicago, New York, and other major cities bear witness to the exoticization of society from within that was just beginning then. The next side street could lead to another world.

The emerging Penny Press showed interest in this social pluralization. It "discovered what was close at hand, but at the same time deviant and curious, as newsworthy material" (Lindner 2007, p. 19). Reporters began to investigate mortuaries, bordellos, factories, and slaughterhouses. Jacob A. Riis (Harper 2012, p. 24 ff.), who emigrated to New York from Denmark, exemplifies this development. The police reporter, who is regarded as the founder of social photojournalism, took pictures of subcultural lifeworlds in Lower Manhattan in the 1880s, which first appeared as illustrations in newspaper and were later published in the photography book *How the Other Half Lives* (1997). Riis shows social realities that are geographically close but culturally far away. His work consists of *ethnographic lifeworld analyses*, mapped spaces and photographic portraits of street boys, Chinese opium smokers, bohemians, and Jews. Riis was however not only an ethnographer, but also a social reformer. His aim was to point out social grievances.

Even more radical were the "girl stunt reporters" who published social reportage in major American daily newspapers in the late 1880s. On commission from the papers, they went undercover to the prisons, factories, and poorhouses of large cities and reported on the abuses there. Elisabeth Cochrane, writing under the pseudonym Nellie Bly, was the most famous representative of this women's movement. In 1887, she had herself admitted to a New York psychiatric clinic. Her report, *Ten Days in a Mad-House* (Bly 2009)—which revealed inhumane conditions and triggered a political scandal—helped develop the participatory, covert practice of undercover research. Lindner points out the reciprocal influence of urban reportage and ethnography (2007, p. 115): Both thematize the foreignness that is found next door; both are explorative and based on experience. This development was anticipated by reporters in the nineteenth century and not taken up by the social sciences until some decades later.

Robert E. Park and Ernest W. Burgess of the Chicago School of sociology understood the metropolis as a laboratory in which human behavior could be investigated (Park and Burgess 1967, p. 1). Within the Chicago School milieu, the primary concern of study was societal marginality: thieves (Sutherland 1989), migrant workers (Anderson 1998), ghettos (Wirth 1998), slums (Zorbaugh 1929), vice (Reckless 1969), ethnically mixed marriages (Adams 1975), or the Italian quarter in Boston (Whyte 1981). Just as in investigative journalism, research was conducted by going undercover. Frances R. Donovan, for instance, worked as a sales girl in a department store for 2 months and wrote a report about it (1988). This tradition was continued by others, such as James P. Spradley, who wrote—among other things—about urban itinerants and alcoholics (1999), the deaf (Spradley and Spradley 1985) and barmaids (Spradley and Mann 1975). The immersive approach was also followed by Loïc Wacquant, who spent several years training at a boxing gym on the South Side of Chicago (2006).

Ethnography aimed to map the processes through which people created their world (Dellwing and Prus 2012, p. 53). The main focus of ethnography is: "What people do, what people know, and the things people make and use" (Spradley 1980, p. 5). Fundamentally, ethnography is an empirical process that involves linguistic, mental, visual, sensory, and corporeal aspects (Pink 2015, p. 26 ff.). To investigate ethnographically means collecting data by exposing oneself—that is, one's own body—to the unpredictable influences of another lifeworld (Coffey 1999, p. 59 ff.; Goffman 1989, p. 125). In contrast to ethnographic field work in anthropology, design ethnography usually takes place in the context of one's "own" society. We do not have to travel like Malinowsky to the Trobriand Islands in order to experience the foreign. A "journey" to a nursing home, or a Thai boxing club, or a hole-in-the-wall bar will lead us to an adventure around the corner.

In this context, George E. Marcus poses the question of whether lifeworlds can still be conceived of as closed, microscopic entities at all, as in Malinowski's work. Marcus proposes a *multi-sited ethnography*, which follows ensembles of people, things, metaphors, scripts, biographies, and conflicts that circulate globally (1995, p. 106 ff.). This may be illustrated with reference to a research project I conducted together with the designer Bitten Stetten on landmine victims, disability, and creative practices in Angola (Müller 2016). The energetic Kuduro music produced, sung, and danced in the *musseque*[1]—the slums in Luanda—is a mixture of western Techno and Angolese Kilapanga and Semba. The long fingernails, rhinestone earrings, and knee socks with flip-flops that we observed on young Kudoro dancers in Sambizanga (a musseque in Luanda) (Stetter 2016, p. 90) are not an isolated phenomenon, but can be read in a global context. Here, elements of a global pop culture are mixed with Angolan culture. Many young people in Angola have a smartphone and a Facebook profile. They know the football stars from Madrid and Barcelona. They are connected with students in Rio de Janeiro and Lisbon. Because socialization still continues to occur in microsocial contexts, however, societies still develop differently as before. This is why a globally uniform culture has not emerged (Tilley 2009, p. 267). Consumer goods and global brands are inculturated, adapted, and imbued with new meanings. For this reason, globalization leads not to uniformity but rather to transformation.

In her understanding of ethnography, Sarah Pink links knowledge gained from field work with individual experience. She defines ethnography "as a process of creating and representing knowledge or ways of knowing that are based on ethnographers' own experiences and the ways these intersect with the persons, places and things encountered during that process" (Pink 2013, p. 35). When we are familiar with a lifeworld, it is all the more challenging not to classify things prematurely and instead to observe the familiar with a phenomenological gaze, which is also referred to as "defamiliarization" (Bell et al. 2006).

5.2 Focused Ethnographies and Design Anthropology

A fundamental distinction may be drawn between classical and focused ethnography (Knoblauch 2006). Classical ethnography in the tradition of the Chicago School is characterized by long-term immersion in the field, openness, and description of impressions and experiences. Focused ethnographies are practiced in applied fields

---

[1]The concept comes from Kimbundu (*Mu-seke*) and means something like a sandy place, which describes the unpaved ground of the Luandan slums (Moorman 2008, p. 32).

such as architecture (Cranz 2016), business and marketing (Salvador et al. 1999), Human Computer-Interaction (HCI) (Bannon and Bødker 1991; Nardi 1993; Suchman 1987) and Computer Supported Cooperative Work (CSCW) (Crabtree et al. 2009; Hughes et al. 1994, 1995; Shapiro 1994). In contrast to the knowledge-oriented classical ethnographies, the goal of focused ethnography consists in the implementation of a new technology, a system design, and artifact, a building, etc. While classical ethnographies are intensive in terms of *time* and *experience*, focused ethnographies are *data-intensive*. Technical recording devices are used to gather detailed data from specific lifeworlds within a relatively brief period of time (Knoblauch 2001, p. 130). Accordingly, these *data-intensive* approaches are also known as "wired ethnography" (Knoblauch 2001, p. 127). In business contexts—for instance, innovation management—ethnographic investigation can take as little as a single or even half a day (Salvador et al. 1999, p. 36).

In the 1980s, the Xerox Palo Alto Research Center in California produced *Workplace Studies*: Lucy A. Suchman intertwined cultural anthropology with engineering in her dissertation, *Plans and Situated Actions: The problem of human-machine communication* (1987), in which she argued that human behavior cannot be determined by machines but that it arises *in situ*. Suchman introduced into technological discourse the ethno-methodological concept of *situated action*, which posits that actions deviate from plans. One of the findings is that human action does not conform to what the engineers conceived but rather follows from specific situations.

In the 1980s, there were some collaborations between anthropologists from the USA and design researchers from Scandinavia (Bloomberg and Karasti 2013, p. 87), where participatory design research had already developed in the late 1960s and early 1970s, as visionary social models and new technologies began to receive more attention (Bjerknes et al. 1987; Kensing and Greenbaum 2013, p. 27 ff.; Mareis et al. 2013). Alison J. Clarke notes that starting as early as 1968, anthropological approaches had already entered into design discourses, which had previously been oriented strongly on industrial productivity (2016, p. 71). This is the environment in which participatory *Action Research* arose (Blomberg and Karasti 2013; Reason 2004; Reason and Bradbury 2008). At that time, designers were conducting workshops with users, testing new technologies, developing mock-ups, and constructing future scenarios. Design ethnography established itself in the 1990s in this rather technology- and market-driven environment (Nova 2014, p. 29 ff.). In the article "Ethnographic Field Methods and Their Relation to Design" Jeanette Blomberg et al. identifies the central reason why ethnography is important when it comes to the implementation of new technologies in workplaces (Blomberg et al. 1993, p. 141 f.): because designers create artifacts for workplace contexts about which they know very little—and will therefore pursue their own needs and conceptions.

This accords with the notion of *User-Centered Design*, which became a topic of discussion in the 1980s (Gould and Lewis 1985): the center is, so to speak, the lifeworld of the user and the "member's point of view," which the researcher closes in on through methods such as on-site observation, informal interviews, and video recording (Blomberg et al. 1993, p. 127 ff.). Hughes et al. described four types of ethnographic approaches (1994, p. 432 ff.)[2] applied in CSCW that also have potential for design ethnography:

- *Concurrent ethnography*: A technical system or a "rapid prototype" is introduced into praxis at the same time as it is observed ethnographically, whereby iterative loops, such as field research—debriefing—design of a prototype—field research, are played through several times. The observations are focused on the human-object or human-interface interactions. This type of research usually lasts a year or a little longer.
- *Quick and dirty ethnography*: This refers primarily to quick forays into the field. Such ethnographies are "dirty" because they are not very detailed. This process can provide an overview of an area that has been defined in advance. Length: 2–3 weeks.
- *Evaluative ethnography*: This ethnography is performed after the implementation of a new technology or system. It is focused. Various forms of interview are utilized as the main method. Length: 2–4 weeks.
- *Re-examination of previous studies*: This refers to analyses of earlier ethnographic studies. It is therefore purely desk research with no visit to the field.

Yana Milev criticizes the kind of applied design research that serves to generate prospering branches of industry and multiple labels as "design governance" (2015, p. 144). In contrast, the design anthropology she proposes places "the complex habitat of cultures as well as the anthropological techniques of constructing meaning and survival at the center of the theory and practice of design" (2015, p. 145).

Keith M. Murphy and George E. Marcus have mapped out the similarities between design and ethnography in social research, which they describe as follows (Murphy and Marcus 2013, p. 257 ff.): (1) *Design and ethnography exist as product and process*, (2) *Design and ethnography are focused on research*, (3) *Design and ethnography are people-centered*, (4) *Design and ethnography are at the service of more than the thing itself*, and (5) *Design and ethnography are reflexive*. At the same time, differences come into play that are related to the fact that design is characterized by being *future oriented*, *interventionist*, and *collaborative* (Otto and Smith 2013, p. 3 f.).

Ethnography in the social sciences is primarily interested in observing the "naturalistic backdrops of foreign groups" (Dellwing and Prus 2012, p. 54 ff.) and deriving theories from this. This is why structured interviews, which are "artificial" situations, are perceived as a problem and "conversations" are preferred (Dellwing and Prus 2012, p. 117). Design intervenes and orients itself on the future, which to some extent it itself creates (Yelavich and Adams 2014). Future, in this context, should be understood less as a linear exploration of the present than as a multitude of ideas, critiques, and possibilities that is embedded in the narrative, objects, and practices of our everyday world (Kjærsgaard et al. 2016, p. 1). In design

---

[2]These four types of ethnographic approaches are also described in Crabtree et al. (2012, p. 77 f.) and Knoblauch (2001, p. 128).

ethnography, situations are disrupted, data is interpreted more quickly, and the processes are iterative. Moreover, fieldwork, analysis, and the transfer to design cannot always be sharply distinguished (Bratteteig et al. 2013, p. 134 f.). In this context, Crabtree et al. posit:

> Fieldwork is not about going out and looking at what people do, gathering some "data," and then analyzing it when you get back to the ranch. Analysis is part and parcel of fieldwork. It permeates fieldwork. When you go into a field—into a setting—you should be doing analysis. (Crabtree et al. 2012, p. 130)

In the context of design ethnography, iterative processes continually produce hypotheses, out of which prototypes, workshops, mock-ups, future scenarios, etc., are developed. Murphy and Marcus postulate that it is not just that design can learn from ethnography, but that enrichment also flows in the other direction: ethnography can also learn from design—for instance, from its iterative, less linear and more playful approach to the field and the data (2013, p. 253 ff.).

The design researcher Nicola Nova provides a descriptive treatment of ethnography in his book *Beyond Design Ethnography. How Designers practice Ethnographic Research* (2014). Nova interviews designers about how they apply the methods in practice. To distinguish design ethnography as compared to ethnography in the social sciences, Nova lists the following characteristics:

> The time spent in the field is shorter, the focus is more narrow, the analysis of the material is closely linked to the design practices with the production of intermediary objects [...], the field data are widely heterogenous, the ways that 'results' are presented are so distinct from anthropology that it's sometimes difficult to draw a clear line between "field results" and "design work". (Nova 2014, p. 117)

Design ethnography is not about a fixation on methods, but rather about immersion in social lifeworlds. Curiosity and a fundamentally open attitude toward people and social lifeworlds is paramount. It is about a radical attentiveness to social realities, whereby the methods for achieving this are only a means and not an end in themselves (Charmaz and Mitchell 2009, p. 161). Crabtree et al. even maintain that methods should be eschewed completely (2012, p. 67), which on a philosophical level accords with the *epistemological anarchism* of Paul Feyerabend (2010). Salvador et al. plead for using methods creatively, by always developing them specifically for an individual field context (1999, p. 41). Nonetheless, there are certain aspects—such as for instance access to the field or the researcher's role in the field—that are relevant to any field research and which will therefore be discussed in more detail in the next sections.

5.3 Access to the Field

To explore a particular lifeworld, it is best to simply go where it is located (this could be a digital as well as a physical space). This, however, might turn out to be a considerable challenge, depending on the place. While there are some lifeworlds that one can simply enter spontaneously, for others—such as for instance "total institutions" (Goffman 1961) such as prisons or mental hospitals—a formal permit would be needed. While certain groups are very accessible, other react to foreign visitors with hostility or even aggression. Robert Prus proposes four ways of accessing the field: (a) *utilizing our own experiences*, (b) *accessing mutual settings*, (c) *finding sponsors*, and (d) *making "cold calls"* (1997, p. 216 ff.).

In each of these cases, it is important to have a gatekeeper—that is, a person who knows the field and is trusted there in ways that can carry over to the ethnographer. The impression one makes when entering the field is also critical. In certain areas, to enter the field without a gatekeeper is dangerous or nearly impossible. For our fieldwork in Angola, we made use of the contacts of a half-Angolese architect with whom I have long been personally acquainted. This man accompanied us during our first 3 days in Luanda and introduced us to important people to whom he had previously reached out—such as leaders of an NGO that assists victims of war and people with disabilities. Together with these officials, we could go into the field and conduct interviews within the local lifeworlds with those who were affected (Müller 2016, p. 69 ff.). In the case of Larissa Holaschke, who investigated the subversive strategies of women in Iran in her master's thesis, couch surfing turned out to be a successful mode of entry into the field. In this manner, Holaschke came into direct contact with people from the liberal-minded milieus that were the focus of her research (2016). She gained direct insight into the lifeworlds and limited spaces of freedom that were found behind closed doors.

The situations looks different when it comes to experiments, focus groups, and interventionist methods such as cultural probes. In those cases, test subjects must be identified in advance. This raises the question—particularly with qualitative methods, which are used with small groups—of what criteria should be used to select them. Nicholas Nova asked designers what process they used to form their test groups and encountered the following methods of selection (Nova 2014, p. 48 f.):

- *Random*: Arbitrary people chosen from the population
- *Homogenous*: A focus group of people with common characteristics
- *Comparative method*: Various groups for comparison
- *Extreme cases*: People and groups with patterns of behavior or characteristics that deviate sharply from the norm
- *According to reputation*: Recruiting test subjects based on recommendation
- *Beyond-users*: non-users or abstainers as a focus group
- *Analog situations*: Focusing on situations similar to what is characteristic for the field being investigated

When selecting test subjects, it is important to consider what is motivating them to participate. In some field work, there may be little understanding for a research project. People in certain environments might not even understand that there is something like a specific research interest in them. If they are willing to collaborate, then, this mainly has to do with a liking for the researcher. Or they may see possible economic advantages in participation, which should be openly discussed and negotiated.

5.4 Researcher's Role in the Field

The researcher's role in the field has been variously handled in anthropology, and there has been no lack of self-critical and occasionally ironic judgment. The anthropologist John van Maanen describes ethnographers as "dull visitors," "meddlesome busybodies," "hopeless dummies," "social creeps," "anthropofoologists," "management spies," and "government dupes" (2011, p. 2). In some societal milieus, anthropology is a foreign concept—and consequently, the presence of researchers in the field can be alienating. The situation in the field thus ceases to be "natural," as the researcher in fact wants it to be. Their presence alters the field.

It is rather rare for designers to conduct fieldwork in Angola or the south of Mexico. Mostly, they operate in environments that are not entirely remote from them. But even those who deal with the milieus of computer games, rock climbing, dementia, or insect eaters are challenged to engage with the genuinely specific aspects of the corresponding lifeworlds and realms of consumption. And if they are no strangers to these worlds—for instance, if they themselves are active gamers—they will attempt to distance themselves artificially.

When I was conducting fieldwork in a Ghanian and a Swiss evangelical community in the greater Zurich area (Müller 2015), I was received openly by both. On my first visit to the Ghanian Sunday service, I was asked to come to the front and introduce myself to the attendees. In the course of my visits, I was able to convince the pastor of the relevance of my research and could move about freely throughout the spaces. However, not everyone was aware of my role as an ethnographer. My attempts to maintain distance at ceremonies such as healings and exorcisms were often ignored by the faithful because they saw me as a potential convert and encouraged me to participate. One day, when I was attending a baptism, a pastor wanted to baptize me alongside. She said I had been there long enough after all and knew enough about the faith. As an agnostic who personally has no use whatsoever for evangelicalism, I of course declined.

Distance and proximity, among other things, are thematized in the sociology of religion in connection with methodological agnosticism. This refers to an attitude that brackets the content of religion as ontological truth. For example, whether religious testimonials—such as conversion narratives—are "true" cannot be determined by the sociologist of religion, but only within the limited social lifeworld of religious practice. There—in the field—is where the "truth" that is of interest to the researcher will be intersubjectively negotiated. For "[...] the task of the ethnographer is not to determine 'the truth' but to reveal the multiple truths apparent in others' lives" (Emerson et al. 1995, p. 3).

Dellwing and Prus note that ethnography has "hot" phases of participation, during which one is passionately involved and contrasting "cooler" phases, in which one is calmer and more distanced (2012, p. 69). Goffman advocates for an immersive approach:

> The sights and sounds around you should get to be normal. You should be able to even play with the people, and make jokes back and forth [...]. The members of the opposite sex

should become attractive to you. You should be able to engage in the same body rhythms, rate of movement, tapping your feet, that sort of thing, as the people around you. (Goffman 1989, p. 129)

This leads to a temporary immersion in specific lifeworld contexts. Ethnographers adapt to situations. They are chameleons. Fieldwork alters them. It is important to set aside one's own values, at least temporarily, and conform to the field. Within intercultural constellations, in particular, one's own convictions and ideologies could become obstacles. For instance, Marimar Sanz Abbul and Mariam Bujalil reported at the MX Design Conference in Mexico City:

> When a group of students from Mexico City visited an indigenous community in the mountains and did not touch the food because it had meat and many of them were vegetarians, the target community's trust toward the class immediately broke down and the project had to be prematurely terminated. (cited in Sierach 2016, p. 57)

Ethnographers should be open, curious, empathetic, adaptable, and ready to revise their opinions, preconceptions, and values—at least to a certain extent. Anne Honer advocates taking people in the field seriously and not overwriting them with one's own moral ideals (2011, p. 87). Those who only judge and are not prepared to reconsider their own opinions are rather unsuitable for ethnographic fieldwork. Salvador et al. therefore write about design ethnography: "We will study people. It's their voice, their story, not our own [...]" (1999, p. 41).

5.5 Observation

Observations are always intentional. We cannot see everything. Our biological make-up does not allow us to see the world in 360°. Even within our field of vision, we only see a portion in sharp focus and the rest is unclear. Maturana and Varela have called attention to the epistemological consequences of this biological structure. They speak of a *blind spot*: "We do not see that we do not see" (2003, p. 8). The gaze is singular, given that it originates in the consciousness of a biological individual whose body is situated in a particular place. Ethnographic observation is always based on selection (Katz 2019).

What do these epistemological considerations mean for ethnographic observation, which Roland Girtler calls the "queen of fieldwork methods" (2001, p. 147)? For one thing, they relativize the faith in objectivity. Objectivity is based on reduction. I can, for instance, count the number of people in a certain space. This number is objective. But this objectivity obscures a universe of other attributes—for example, the gender, age, ethnicity, etc., of the people in the room, the clothes they are wearing, their behavior, whether they are meditating, sitting on chairs, boxing, working at computers, dancing, etc. Obviously, I can operationalize each of these individual attributes in turn. I can quantify the gender, ethnicity, age, etc. and capture these statistically, but this does not overcome the basic problem that objectivity is attained only through reductionism. Seeing is thus always a form of classification. Seeing is based on prior knowledge:

> We, people of today, directly see a railroad station, a form that a primitive man would be unable to see. He would look at the mass of ironwork in tangled "laths" fixed to the ground, at houses on wheels, at a hard-breathing monster exhaling fire and smoke, and he would probably see his own forms: the dragon, the devil, perhaps many other things, but not our good old railway. (Fleck 1986, p. 137)

When we observe ethnographically, then, we should attempt to set aside such acquired knowledge, at least partially. In this process, the familiar is particularly problematic because it is classified all too rapidly. That is why Manfred Lueger calls for the familiar and the mundane to be transformed into an unfamiliar state "by decomposing it, treating it as something new, looking for conceivable connections of meaning" (Lueger 2000, p. 111).

5.6 Dimensions of Observation

On epistemological grounds, then, we cannot see everything and therefore always define a focus. Lueger distinguishes three possible areas of focus in observation (2000, p. 107 ff.): (1) *actors*, (2) *events and actions*, (3) *objects and products*. These three dimensions can be used to describe any social situation, since they are found in all of them. There are people involved who are carrying out actions (even if they are passively meditating, that is an action) and there are always objects—for instance clothing—on hand. Even in places where people are naked—doctor's offices, swinger clubs, and nude beaches—there are culturally specific objects present. James P. Spradley descries ethnographic observation as follows: "We observe what people do (cultural behavior); we observe things people make and use such as clothes and tools (cultural artifacts); and we listen to what people say (speech messages)" (Spradley 1980, p. 10).

Spradley differentiates between *grand tour observations* and *mini-tour observations* (1980, p. 77 ff.). He compares grand tour observations with a tour of a house, a school, or a business, in which someone is shown the basic structure of the building. If one then goes into the individual rooms and examines them, to stick with the building metaphor, then those are *mini-tour observations*. Spradley emphasizes that the observations are actually made in an identical manner, but the main difference is that the focus is on units of a different scale. He distinguishes between nine dimensions of observation (1980, p. 78):

- *Space*: the physical place
- *Actor*: the people involved
- *Activity*: a set of various actions
- *Object*: the physical things
- *Act*: individual acts carried out by the people
- *Event*: a set of activities carried out by the people

- *Time*: the chronological sequence
- *Goal*: the aims people wish to accomplish
- *Feeling*: the emotions that are expressed

Spradley is interested in the interactions between the nine dimensions, which he presents in his *descriptive question matrix* (1980, pp. 82–83), which results in 81 fields (Table 5.1).

These 81 fields create a grid that is an effective way of bringing to light the complexity in a social situation on the one hand and reducing it analytically on the other. Along the diagonal line of the matrix, where the same two categories meet, is where the detailed description of that category takes place—which Spradley calls the "grand tour questions" (1980, p. 81). Next to this, in the fields in which the interdependencies between the various dimensions are investigated, are the "mini-tour questions" (Spradley 1980, p. 81). Such a matrix can be helpful in looking for certain dimensions. It could be used to more closely examine a relevant focus—for instance, time, objects, or emotions. This focus might arise during the fieldwork, or it could already be determined in advance. If the design project consists in creating a new object, it makes most sense to intensively investigate all the questions that are related to objects.

5.7 Front and Back Regions

Goffman called attention to some other dimensions relevant for observation: A setting has what he called a *front* and a *back stage* (Goffman 1956, p. 66 ff.), which should be understood as relational and not substantive entities. The classic example is in the theater. While on the front region of the stage, the actors play a specific role and are exposed to a great degree of scrutiny, backstage they act more relaxed, make jokes, or rest. This is similar in expensive restaurants: there, the servers behave toward the guests in accordance with particular rules, while back in the kitchen the interaction is gruff. The servers alter their behavior depending on the space in which they find themselves. The speak a different language, use different words, carry themselves differently, etc. In short, place determines social identity.

These categories are, as mentioned, relational. If we define the church service as the front stage, then the bible study group can be defined as back stage. At the front stage, normative identities are constituted through sermons, while in the bible group, as a back stage, communication can be personal and intimate (Müller 2015, p. 146 ff.). Within the bible group itself there are also front and back stages. The front stage, for instance, can be the entire space in which interaction happens among the group. The back stage could be the kitchen, where snacks are being prepared, or the office where the bible group is organized. The theatrical metaphor suggests that the identity on the front stage should be seen as "played" while the one back stage is "authentic." But in American Pragmatism and symbolic interaction theory there is no such thing

5.7 Front and Back Regions

Table 5.1 Spradley's descriptive question matrix

	Space	Object	Act	Activity
Space	Can you describe in detail all the *places*?	What are all the ways space is organized by objects?	What are all the ways space is organized by acts?	What are all the ways space is organized by activities?
Object	Where are objects located?	Can you describe in detail all the *objects*?	What are all the ways objects are used in acts?	What are all the ways objects are used in activities?
Act	Where do acts occur?	How do acts incorporate the use of objects?	Can you describe in detail all the *acts*?	How are acts part of activity?
Activity	What are all the places activities occur?	What are all the ways activities incorporate objects?	What are all the ways activities incorporate acts?	Can you describe in detail all the activities?
Event	What are all the places events occur?	What are all the ways events incorporate objects?	What are all the ways events incorporate acts?	What are all the ways events incorporate activities?
Time	Where do time periods occur?	What are all the ways time affects objects?	How do acts fall into time period?	How do activities fall into time period?
Actor	Where do actors place themselves?	What are all the ways actors use objects?	What are all the ways actors use acts?	How are actors involved in activities?
Goal	Where are goals sought and achieved?	What are all the ways goals involve use of objects?	What are all the ways goals involve acts?	What activities are goal seeking or linked to goals?
Feeling	Where do the various feeling states occur?	What feelings lead to the use of what objects?	What are all the ways feeling affect acts?	What are the ways feelings affect activities?

Event	Time	Actor	Goal	Feeling
What are all the ways space is organized by events?	What spatial changes occur over time?	What are all the ways space is used by actors?	What are all the ways space is related to goals?	What places are associated with feelings?
What are all the ways objects are used in events?	How are objects used in different times?	What are all the ways objects are used by actors?	How are objects used in seeking goals?	What are the ways objects evoke feelings?
How are acts a part of events?	How do acts vary over time?	What are the ways acts are performed by actors?	What are all the ways acts are related to goals?	What are all the ways acts are linked to feelings?
What are all the ways activities are parts of events?	How do activities vary at different times?	What are all the ways activities involve actors?	What are all the ways activities involve goals?	How do activities involve feelings?
Can you describe in detail all the *events*?	How do events occur over time? Is there any sequencing?	How do events involve the various actors?	How are events related to goals?	How do events involve feelings?

(continued)

Table 5.1 (continued)

Event	Time	Actor	Goal	Feeling
How do events fall into time period?	Can you describe in detail all the *times*?	When are all the times actors are "on stage"?	How are goals related to time periods?	When are feelings evoked?
How are actors involved in events?	How do actors change over time or at different times?	Can you describe in detail all the *actors*?	Which actors are linked to which goals?	What are the feelings experienced by actors?
What are all the ways events are linked to goals?	Which goals are scheduled for which times?	How do the various goals affects the various actors?	Can you describe in detail all the *goals*?	What are all the ways goals evoke feelings?
What are the ways feelings affect events?	How are feelings related to various time periods?	What are the ways feelings involve actors?	What are the ways feelings influence goals?	Can you describe in detail all the *feelings*?

as "authentic" identity. Identity is always produced through naming and classification (Strauss 2017, p. 17 ff.)—and is therefore contingent.

A situation will not necessarily be conclusively understood through observation alone, which is why ambiguities might be cleared up through interviews (Honer 2011, p. 31).That observation can have its limits is something I would like to illustrate by an example from my own fieldwork, which involved a visit to the Sunday service at a Ghanian evangelical church in Zurich (Müller 2015, p. 122). It was Pentecost, and the mood of the worshippers was excited from the start. The pastor invoked the Holy Spirit. He called on everyone—including me—to come up front, where we all stood close together in a semicircle. He went from one to another and put his hand on their brow. One woman at the start fell to the ground and began to speak in tongues. Other women followed. The mood was ecstatic. Then a young woman walked quite calmly up to the front. She seemed completely untouched by the ecstatic mood. She did not fall to ground after the pastor laid hands on her, but rather lay down gently and slowly. Finally, she lay motionless on her stomach while another woman put a white cloth on her back. I could describe these actions, but the meaning was not conclusive. Why were there such obviously different reactions to the workings of the Holy Spirit? Why did it have an ecstatic effect on most, while this young woman was contemplative in behavior? At a later point, I asked the pastor about this situation. He explained to me that the Holy Spirit manifests in different ways. If a person twitches sharply after the laying on of hands, as most women did, then this indicates a conflict taking place inside them between evil spirits and the Holy Spirit. The young woman who lay down calmly did not have any evil spirits inside her—and accordingly, the Holy Spirit manifested itself gently. The Holy Spirit could even be at work while someone was deeply asleep. Only now did another observation that I had made repeatedly for some time finally become conclusive. I had seen people sleeping in the service. That this sleep had religious connotation would not have become evident from pure observation alone.

5.8 Interviews and Conversations

When situations do not become conclusive on the basis of observation, interviews and conversations are then warranted for clarification. I use the two terms consciously, since they refer to two different types of face-to-face communication. The interview arose during the nineteenth century in the context of American journalism. Crime beat reporters working on human interest stories began to orient themselves on police interrogation and incorporated quotations from them into their texts. Interviewing as a method of social science became established only later.

Question-answer situations are based on the assumption that there are disparities in knowledge (if this were not that case, there would be no reason to ask the questions). Furthermore, social science interviews are artificial situations that do not exist in everyday communication—similar to confession, psychoanalytic talk therapy, or police interrogation. These settings are subject to certain framings and power dynamics that are more (police interrogation) or less (psychoanalysis) explicit, raising various questions: What does the interviewee hope for? What are their goals and motivations for participating in the interview? Does the interviewee understand the role in which they are being addressed in the interview? Has the interviewee agreed to audio recording of the interview?

In principle, interviews in the social sciences are divided into *qualitative* and *quantitative*, *open* and *structured* types, in which *soft* and *hard* and *open* and *closed* questions can be asked. In the context of ethnographic interviews, it is important to ask open rather than closed questions—that is, the questions should be able to open up new horizons and not simply be answered with a yes or no (Liebold and Trinczek 2009, p. 38).

In the qualitative context, there are *focused interviews* (Flick 2014, p. 211 ff.; Merton 1987), *semi-structured interviews* (Flick 2014, p. 217 ff.), *problem-centered Interviews* (Flick 2014, p. 223 ff.) and *expert interviews* (Flick 2014, p. 227 ff.), which require extensive preparation and are therefore described by Michaela Pfadenhauer as a "conversation between an expert and a quasi-expert" (2002). Further, there are *narrative* (Schütze 1983) and *ethnographic* interviews (Spradley 1979), which will be discussed later. Another distinction concerns *classic* and *idealist* approaches to interviews, where subjects present their real lifeworlds and experiences in the former, and their wishes in the latter (Byrne 2012, p. 208).

Video recording of interviews is generally discouraged because this can negatively impact that atmosphere of the conversation. Whenever possible, interviews should be documented through audio recording, since no one can take notes and conduct a conversation at the same time. Of course, recording is not always possible, and especially with informal conversations, a recorder can be disturbing to the interlocutor. Turning on the recording mode on a smart phone can equally lead to a break—from that point on, conversations often become suddenly formal and "artificial," although this feeling may dissipate after a short time. I have often had the experience in interviews that after the recording device is turned off—that is, as soon as the formal part is over—this is when the interviewee really begins to tell the story. Such situations demonstrate how strongly the technology impacts our behavior.

In any case, the interviewer needs the competence "*to understand roles*, to grasp 'as who' he himself is seen and 'as who' his interlocutor acts and speaks" (Hermanns 2008, p. 364). Harry Hermanns describes the interview as a drama that is substantially shaped by the interviewer. He offers the following stage directions (2008, p. 367):

- The framework and objectives of the interview should be made transparent to the interviewee through a briefing.
- A pleasant atmosphere should be created during the interview.
- The interviewee should be given space to show several aspects of themselves. If the interviewer is embarrassed by anything, they should make clear that they will not avoid the content and subject.
- The drama must be allowed to develop. This is facilitated by posing brief and easily understandable questions about the lifeworld of the interviewee. Jargon should not be used.
- The conversation should not explore any theoretical concepts but rather focus on the lifeworld of the interviewee. This also means that the interviewer should ask follow-up questions if something is unclear and allow the interviewee to explain situations with precision.

5.9 Narrative Interview

The narrative interview was developed by the German sociologist Fritz Schütze. This type of interview deals primarily with autobiographical aspects and themes (Svasek and Domencka 2012). In the narrative interview process, the initial question is particularly significant: it should induce the freest possible narrative flow, upon which the interviewer should step back so as not to disturb it. The narrative interview is divided into three phases (Schütze 1983, p. 285):

- *Narrative prompt*: The prompt can refer to the entire biography or can be focused on a specific phase of life—for instance, a religious conversion, an illness, or a period of unemployment. This initial question should be formulated openly and not be suggestive. The interviewee marks the end of this sequence with phrases such as "so, that was it."
- *Immanent follow-up questions*: Here the interviewer takes up certain statements from the initial narrative and probes them with deeper questions. It is important that these follow up questions, too, are open and evoke new narrative flows.

- *Exmanent follow-up questions*: Here, the interviewer will introduce their own topics of interest into the interview that have not yet been discussed. These questions may relate to other interviews or theoretical knowledge.

A narrative interview lasts at least an hour. Whether the initial question will actually be sufficient to set the narrative flow in motion depends on a number of factors—the mutual sympathy between the two interlocutors (narrative interviews should be conducted in private, since people open up significantly more to just one listener); the interviewee's trust in the interviewer; the situation and place where the interview is conducted; the negotiated timeframe; the agreed-upon conditions of anonymity; and cultural influences. It should be noted in this context that interviews do not represent realities but rather reconstruct them narratively. Thus, they are not mirror reflections of events and experiences (Hahn 1995, p. 140).

5.10 Ethnographic Interviews

Roland Girtler criticizes the narrative interview because in his view the researcher's initial question puts the interviewee on the spot. Moreover, interviews are designed to elicit specific information as quickly and pointedly as possible, which also puts pressure on the interviewee (2001, p. 147 f.). Girtler instead suggests the *ero-epic dialogue*, "in which the point is narratives and stories that might refer to pretty much anything within a culture or group" (Girtler 2001, p. 147). Anne Honer, in turn, speaks of the *explorative interview*, which is intended to open up "the widest possible, 'unknown' and latent areas of the interviewee's knowledge" (2011, p. 41). These approaches resemble the *ethnographic interview* (Maeder 1995, p. 66 f.; Spradley 1979). This type of interview is characterized by the idea "that *the researcher must first learn from their informants* what the right questions to pose even are" (Maeder 1995, p. 66). Ethnographic interviews begin as open interviews and become increasingly more closed. In this way, hypotheses are developed during an interview through an abductive process that are then woven into new questions. Spradley emphasizes that ethnographic interviews are quite similar to "friendly conversations": "It is best to think of ethnographic interviews as a series of friendly conversations into which the researcher slowly introduces new elements to assist informants to respond as informants" (Spradley 1979, p. 58).

The place where a conversation or interview takes place is important. Is it happening within the lifeworld being investigated or is it in a "laboratory setting"—for instance, in a seminar room at a university? The proponents of the laboratory setting argue that this "neutral" environment helps to clarify connections more precisely. This however begs the question of how "neutral" a laboratory—such as a seminar room—actually is. Most likely, "there are no decontextualized, that is, 'pure,' interview situations" (Liebold and Trinczek 2009, p. 40). One does not go into an interview as a neutral quantity; rather, one has a habitus, a biographical background, a gender, etc. Clothes, hairstyles, and habitus also convey symbolic information that influence the course of the interview.

Conversations situated within the lifeworld under investigation enable direct reference to the things on hand. Daniel Miller has demonstrated this with his study of objects in one hundred apartments in a London street and their biographical significance for the inhabitants (2008). Because there are certain things present in the context of every lifeworld, one can refer to them in a conversation. At the same time, however, there may be other people present as well, who may influence the interviewee's portrayals. It is possible that the respondent may not articulate certain sentiments when people from their personal milieu are there within earshot. During our fieldwork in Angola it was quite disconcerting for us to speak with disabled people while their friends and family were around. It contradicted our conception of the private sphere.

A meeting within the lifeworld context of the interviewee develops an entirely different atmosphere. The conversation develops quite differently when one is drinking or eating together. Even the question of whether one sits together at a table or stays on the move—for instance, while taking a tour of a building or a home or taking a walk—produces a different kind of conversation. A walk with a person on their own familiar territory shows how people adapt to spaces (Holliday 2007, p. 256; Kusenbach 2008; Lee and Ingold 2006; Pink 2007b, p. 240 ff.). This provides information about the "native's view point" (Geertz 1999), which refers not to the subjective individual consciousness, but rather to the cultural grammar with which people access their world.

5.11 The Senses

In western societies, it is assumed that we have five senses: seeing, hearing, smell, taste, and touch. This classification, however—which goes back to Aristotle—is not in fact universal. In her research with the Ewe in Ghana, Kathryn Lin Geurts found terms that denote perceptions that are at once psychological and physical, suggesting that the duality of mind and body that shapes western thought does not exist there (2002, p. 197). If there are cultural differences in how other societies classify the senses, then this has consequences for perception (Pink 2015, p. 59 ff.). This draws attention to a problem inherent to any engagement with questions of sensory perception: We experience the world sensorially, but are not able to express these personal perceptions through language because in doing so we always operate with reference to an already given language and cultural classification. Neither can sensory perception be measured (Pink 2015, p. 136). One can merely attempt to describe it, which is a genuinely interpretive process.

Quite likely, it is these epistemological difficulties of dealing with the sensorily perceptible world that have contributed to making an "Anthropology of the Senses" (Howes 1991) a marginal phenomenon for a long time. The idea has however received more attention recently.[3] Different places have specific olfactory and sound environments. A hospital, a Catholic church, a used book shop, a boxing gym, an Irish pub, a Mexican taqueria—they all have their own specific smell. Objects have scents too—not just food, but also books, furniture, laundry, the interiors of cars. Things have their own haptics, which we experience through touch (Classen 2005), and their own acoustics (Vokes 2007). Smells, scents, and stench are everyday experiences that help us ascribe things to categories such as dirty and clean, which are anthropological ordering schemes (Douglas 1966). In this respect, a description of subjective sensory perceptions in the context of an ethnographic study must be understood less as a representation of an experience and rather more as part of a cultural classification system, in which the researcher themself is embedded. The assumption is that the relevant classifications are a fundamental part of the culture. To research such "sensory categories" (Pink 2015, p. 148 ff.) interactive and participatory processes in which the researcher themself plays a part are most suitable.

In this regard, Sarah Pink speaks of a "multisensory approach" (2011), "digital-visual-sensory-design anthropology" (2014), and "sensory ethnography" (2015). Arantes and Rieger also speak of sensory ethnography (2014).[4] Pink calls attention to the fact that subjective as well as intersubjective sensibility have their relevance (2015, p. 62). Subjective sensibility refers to the personal perception of the researcher. Intersubjective signifies that this experience of the researcher is embedded within a cultural context and within social relationships. Since the "translation" of sensory experience into text entails the aforementioned difficulties, Pink proposes to carry out interventions (2007a, 2015, p. 7). By this, she means events such as jointly producing a film, cooking a recipe, or singing a song with the participants: "The practice of eating food prepared by people with whom one is doing research (or preparing food with or for them) is an obvious way to participate in their everyday lives" (Pink 2015, p. 108).

Harold Garfinkel's "breaching experiments," in which everyday norms were shaken, are worth recalling in this connection. Drawing on this tradition, Kelvin E. Y. Low conducted a study about gender and scent in which he sprayed himself with women's perfume and questioned his social milieu about it (2005, p. 407). At the methodological level, Inga Reimers proposes three approaches to investigating sensory experience (2014, p. 85 ff.):

- *Ethno-mimesis*: Developed by Maggie O'Neill and Phil Hubbard, *Ethno-Mimesis* (2010) aims to produce sensory knowledge through creative means. O'Neill und Hubbard have implemented this approach with asylum seekers, with whom they

---

[3]Noteworthy in this context, for instance, is the Master's thesis of Priscille Jotzu (2018), who aims to convey future scenarios with scents. https://digitaltag.zhdk.ch/en/conference/masterclasses/masterclass-10-smell-o-topia/ (accessed 4 July 2019).

[4]See also the *Sensory Ethnography Lab* at Harvard University (Cambridge, MA): https://sel.fas.harvard.edu (accessed 4 July 2019).

walked together on city streets and spoken with immediately afterward about their experiences.
- *Experimental procedures*: Researchers plan and realize specific settings together. This might, for instance, be a meal in which eating practices are investigated, where feelings are articulated and exchanged. This open-ended and experimental process helps make internalized classification patterns explicit.
- *Situational group discussions*: Researchers create multi-sensory settings—such as a meal—and involve specific groups of test subjects with whom group discussions are then held afterward. The hierarchies between the researchers and the subjects should be as flat as possible.

5.12 Things and Material Culture

Whether we are in a library, a laboratory, a department store, or a museum—we are surrounded by man-made, designed objects. We have internalized implicit knowledge of how to deal with these things and our handling of them is complex and variable: We buy them, use them, consume them, repair them, alter them, throw them away, destroy them. The things in question can be very simple or highly technologically complex. Flatware, for instance, is technically simple—from a cultural perspective, however, even a technically simple fork can turn out to be very complex: "Once a more or less consistent functional core develops and, importantly, becomes historically stable, then forks begin to vary with cultural standards" (Böhme 2012, p. 102). The fact that even something like a mechanical toaster is complex has been demonstrated by Thomas Thwaites in his "Toaster Project" (2011). He obtained and processed his own raw materials and used them to build a replica of a mass-produced toaster by hand. In this way he made visible the complexity of mass-produced objects. What is already a very time-consuming process in the case of a toaster would be completely impossible with a smartphone. In under a decade, smartphones have fundamentally altered the way we communicate, interact, behave in private and public, indeed how we *live* (Bell and Kuipers 2018; Ictech 2019). Virtually no one who uses a smartphone knows how it actually functions technologically. Neither is this necessary, given that it fully suffices to just know how to use it in everyday life. It is only in a crisis—that is, when the smartphone stops working—that the complexity normally concealed by its smart interface is revealed (Berger and Luckmann 1967, p. 24; Latour 2002, p. 223; Schön 1983, p. 59 ff.).

Every society has its own material culture, which is variously dealt with in anthropology (Appadurai 1986; Böhme 2012; Clarke 2017; Habermas 1999; Hahn 2014, 2015; Hahn and Schmitz 2018; Lueger and Froschauer 2018; Miller 2008, 2009a; Müller 2019; Tilley 2009; Tilley et al. 2013). The microcosms of small social lifeworlds are filled with a variety of things: The things inside a Buddhist temple are different from the ones in a Catholic church or a mosque—even though all these places contain both holy and mundane objects. The things in a Kung Fu school are

5.13 Consumption Is Not Superficial   51

different from the ones in a boxing club. A lab contains different things than a law office. A Korean restaurant has different things than a Spanish one. Things in a bathroom are different from the kitchen. At the same time, there are objects that are present in all of these places: for instance, screws, lightbulbs, light switches, etc.

Things have certain material properties. They can be hard, soft, elastic, rough, smooth, matte, bright, light, heavy, etc. Their existence is conditional (Lueger and Froschauer 2018, p. 65 ff.): They have been produced under specific circumstances and in specific contexts. They have functions and meanings, whereby the latter have less to do with their material properties but rather rest on social attributions. We own some things that have a particular meaning for us and others of which we take no notice. We do not pay the same degree of attention to all things—significantly more to a smartphone than to a screw, although screws are certainly fundamental. Some things—such as toothbrushes, towels, or sheets—are a part of our completely private sphere, and accordingly we do not like to share them with other people. Habermas describes these things as our "identity kit" (1999, p. 122 f.). Living spaces contain collections of personal things that manifest a certain lifestyle and individuality. Hartmut Böhme describes them as "storehouse and performative organ of the self" (2012, p. 99). We own things that have a special emotional significance because of their biographical connections—so-called "memory objects" (Hahn 2014, p. 37 ff.). These include souvenirs, which embody an extraordinary experience and evoke a temporally or geographically distanced perspective (Habermas 1999, p. 291 ff.). Family heirlooms transcend the here and now in a similar way. They "lend a social (family) identity, distinction, and belonging, as well as historical identity" (Habermas 1999, p. 292). What we value emotionally is dependent not just on economic value, but also on the habitus and cultural milieu in which we move, our age, the historical era in which we live, etc. At the same time, our personal relationship to things cannot be explained by sociological factors alone, since the relationships that a person has with such things is highly individual.

Things are designed, produced, adapted, further developed, appropriated for different purposes—the latter known as "non-intentional design": being used in a way that the designer did not intend. Such is the case, for instance, when I keep my pens and pencils in a beer glass. Furthermore, objects can also be used as markers to reserve personal space. Sun glasses and a tube of sun block signal someone's claim to a lounge chair on the beach; a drink on the bar lays claim to the bar stool in front of it (Goffman 2010, p. 41). The idea then is that all people practice design and therefore have design knowledge (Cross 2007, p. 47).

5.13 Consumption Is Not Superficial

In the age of modern consumption, a critique of consumerism has also been established to shed some critical light on it. A central argument of this critique has to do with the distinction between (necessary) basic needs and (superfluous) luxury needs. According to this critique, which has gained strength in recent years in sufficiency discourses, we consume more than we truly need. Wasteful, excessive consumption must be disciplined. A further critique claims the objects of consumption are superficial, suggesting that there is a deep inner self that has been coopted by external, "superficial" things. The sociological Frankfurt School and French poststructuralism in particular have branded consumer culture as superficial in judgments dripping with the sort of morality one would sooner expect from puritanical lay preachers than from sociologists.

Daniel Miller rightly points out that the emergence of mass consumption has also greatly contributed to reducing poverty (2013, p. 341). The distinction between things that are *necessary* and *superfluous* is not a universal one; rather, it goes back to puritanical Protestant values (Hahn 2014, p. S78 ff.; Campbell 1998, p. 238). It is in this context that Miller speaks of the *Poverty of Morality* (2011): Anyone who judges one lifestyle to be "wrong" implicitly considers another to be "right." Positions critical of consumerism are less concerned with analyzing the facts of a situation than with branding consumption. As the ethnologist Hans Peter Hahn points out: "On the one hand, the line between luxury and need is subject to an emic, culturally dependent definition; on the other, the European concept of need is influenced by a very particular rhetoric [...]" (Hahn 2014, p. 81). This also contradicts Maslow's pyramid of needs and the mechanistic conception of man associated with it, which posits that self-actualization becomes a goal only after material, rudimentary, and social needs have been met. In his essay "Why Clothing is not Superficial" (2009b), Daniel Miller shows that everyday and consumer culture shapes identity to a great degree and is anything but trivial. Miller debunks the assumption—which is particularly wide-spread in the German-speaking world, that superficiality is a distraction from something deeper:

> We possess what could be called a *depth ontology*. The assumption is that *being*—what we truly are—is located deep inside ourselves and is in direct opposition to the surface. A clothes shopper is shallow because a philosopher or a saint is deep. (Miller 2009b, p. 16)

Consumer goods do not simply satisfy needs; rather, they convey symbolic statements. Mary Douglas and Baron Isherwood have fundamentally refuted the theory of consumption as the satisfaction of need, which is grounded in economics:

> Instead of supposing that goods are primarily needed for subsistence plus competitive display, let us assume that they are needed for making visible and stable the categories of culture. It is standard ethnographic practice to assume that all material possessions carry social meanings and to concentrate a main part of cultural analysis upon their use as communicators. (Douglas and Isherwood 1978, p. 62)

To define eating, drinking, clothing, etc. simply as the satisfaction of need assumes a mechanistic model of mankind and obscures symbolic categories. Douglas describes the manner in which we nourish ourselves as an information system (Douglas 2011, p. 82 ff.). We define ourselves through eating: from *veganism* to *from-nose-to-tail*, whether one's eating habits are ascetic and self-disciplined or hedonistic and pleasure-oriented makes a social statement. Clothing also significantly constructs a social identity, which is why it is also described as a "social skin" (Turner 1980). We are different people when we walk around town in scruffy jeans or in a suit. We make a different impression and experience the world differently. The things with which we surround ourselves form our identity. Accordingly, Habermas posits that clothing is experienced as a part of our person that defines our physical boundaries (1999, p. 67). Mary Douglas describes our entire everyday world as meaningful and symbolically loaded: "we do not seize upon as theatrical props to dramatize the way we want to play our roles and the scene we are playing in" (Douglas 1966, p. 101).

5.14 The Contingency of Things

Anselm Strauss write: "An object which looks so much like an orange—in fact which really is an orange—can also be a member of an infinite number of other classes" (2017, p. 22). An orange can be the fruit of a citrus plant from the Rutaceae family. It can be a food source rich in vitamins. It can be sold as a product in a supermarket or an informal street market. It can be used as the subject of a still life at an art school. At the Basel Carneval it can serve as a projectile, while at the Día de los Muertos in Mexico, it is an offering for the dead. An orange can thus be an object of biology, nourishment, economics, religion, etc. Its identity is contingent, which contradicts the concept of identity that posits that a thing is one. The definitiveness of naming thus brings into the world the contingency that it seeks to overcome. At the same time, the orange has an undeniable materiality. As soon as we begin to describe this materiality in more detail, however, a field of ambiguity opens up again: Do we describe the orange only on the basis of its external appearance? Do we limit ourselves only to its size, color, and form? Do we cut it open, which again produces a different image? Do we squeeze the juice out of it? Do we describe only the isolated orange or do we consider that it grows on a tree that needs water, light, and air? The questions proliferate. This demonstrates that material culture is far more ambiguous than it appears to us in daily life. Or, as Böhme puts it: "Things are deeply familiar to us. When we want to know what they are, they become alien" (2012, p. 35).

5.15 Field Notes

As previously discussed, observation is based on selection: We make decisions, in part conscious ones and in part intuitive. We make further decisions when we take notes. What do we note down? When do we take notes? Do we write notes using key words or complete sentences? What does it actually mean to "translate" an observation into a textual note? Is it a translation or a construction of something new? And why do we take notes at all when we can simply photograph or film the situations in the field with a smart phone?

To begin with, it is important to recognize that working with visual data is fundamentally different from taking notes. Which approach one chooses, or whether one combines several, depends on the research project, its context, and one's personal preferences. It should be kept in mind that notes do not just *describe* actions—rather, the taking of notes is itself an action (Emerson et al. 1995, p. 15).

Emerson et al. speak of "jottings," which build the foundation for "full notes" (1995, p. 51). Spradley calls these brief notations, which are composed of key words rather than fully composed sentences, "condensed accounts" (1980, p. 69). He recommends composing "expanded accounts" immediately after the fieldwork and keeping a "fieldwork journal" in which not only observations but also feelings, associations, and impressions are articulated. The last step is writing up the "analyses and interpretation," which is the final ethnographic report (Spradley 1980, p. 69 ff.).

Taking notes can unsettle people in the field. When we take notes we are signaling that
we consider a situation or a statement significant, which the people in the field may see differently. Goffman therefore recommends not writing notes down during the observation itself, because people would then know which actions were being documented (Goffman 1989, p. 130). This raises the question of whether such evasive tactics are necessary. Ultimately, acceptance of note-taking naturally depends on the field itself and not least on the situations in which one finds oneself. For instance, if you are conducting participant observation of gang members, it will be difficult to take notes during a fight. I had more luck in my fieldwork in the Ghanaian evangelical church community in Zurich: there, many of the worshippers took notes on the pastor's sermons during the Sunday service. In that context, my behavior conformed to the norm—to such an extent, indeed, that many of the attendees took me for a convert.

5.16 Sketches and Illustrations

Sketching is often done so automatically by designers that it is not even perceived as a method of fieldwork. In fact, sketching—called "graphic anthropology" (Tondeur 2016)—is a highly useful approach in fieldwork, especially in situations where photography and video recording is not possible. The designer Franz James employed this method in an investigation of prisons in South Africa, where photography is not allowed (2016, p. 163). Sketching has various advantages (Tondeur 2016, p. 666). First, paper and pencil are cheap. Second—in marked contrast to electronic media—it leads to a more relaxed form of observation. Third, it is considerably less intrusive than photography or filming. And fourth, it often leads to conversations and new forms of encounter in the field. The anthropologist Michael Taussig made the sketches he produced over decades of fieldwork in Columbia into a springboard for the autoethnographic and literary reconstructions in his book *I Swear I Saw This*. Taussig writes: "[...] photography is a *taking*, the drawing a *making* [...]" (2011, p. 21). This active element of sketching leads to more sensitivity and openness in perception. Sketching and drawing can be made by the researcher themselves or—in a participatory approach—by the people within a certain field (Pink 2015, p. 89 f.) Forgoing audiovisual technology leads to more contemplative observation in the field.

5.17 Photography and Video

With smartphones now omnipresent, an enormous amount of visual data is created every day, which is shared, evaluated, commented on, adapted, filtered, deleted, or archived. In 2017, 1.8 trillion photographs were produced, 85% of these with smartphones.[5] According to the German portal *statistica*, 3.26 billion people worldwide had a smartphone in 2019 and the number is projected to reach 3.76 billion in 2021.[6] With 5G technology, upload speeds will become massively faster again, which will significantly increase the production of visual data. But it is not just the quantity but also the quality that is fundamentally changing. Many companies that never had an infrastructure for traditional land-line communication are leaping directly from face-to-face oral interaction into the digital world. In the future, smartphones will be even cheaper and more widely distributed globally, which will further increase the production of photos and video. Ultimately, the smartphone alters not only our culture of interaction and communication, but also the presence and meaning of visuality in our everyday world (Eberle 2017b, p. 111).

This development lends a new relevance to the *Iconic Turn* (Boehm 1994). The new visual worlds require new methodological approaches. Social science journals such as *Visual Ethnography*[7] or *Visual Studies*,[8] which is published by the *International Visual Sociology Association*[9] (IVSA), deal with these visual approaches. Despite the flood of images, visual data in sociology continue to stand in the shadow of text. Aside from visual sociology (Harper 2012) and videography (Knoblauch 2006; Schnettler and Raab 2012; Tuma et al. 2013), visual data in sociology often have merely a documentary function: they supplement texts, which continue to stand at the center. Thomas S. Eberle attributes this to the dominance of positivism in the foundational ideas of sociology, which must be called into question by a turn to the image. He calls attention to the fact that

---

[5] https://blog.wiwo.de/look-at-it/2017/09/14/12-billionen-digitale-fotos-werden-allein-2017-geschossen-davon-85-prozent-per-smartphone/ (accessed 4 July 2019).

[6] https://de.statista.com/statistik/daten/studie/309656/umfrage/prognose-zur-anzahl-der-smartphone-nutzer-weltweit/ (accessed 4 July 2019).

[7] http://www.vejournal.org/index.php/vejournal (accessed 4 July 2019).

[8] https://www.tandfonline.com/toc/rvst20/current (accessed 8 August 2019).

[9] http://visualsociology.org (accessed 4 July 2019).

images have to be interpreted by recipients and due to their more open horizon of interpretive possibility as compared to verbal descriptions always produce a surfeit of meaning. Images can therefore never be fully represented or substituted by text. Conversely, due to their ambiguity and the need for them to be interpreted, images also cannot provide any definitive statement that can be verified intersubjectively. (Eberle 2017a, p. 20)

Anthropology is more open to images than sociology, and accordingly it has long since developed a visual tradition (Harper 2012, p. 5). The anthropologist Bronislaw Malinowski took many photographs during his investigations on the Trobriand Islands (1932). Gregory Bateson and Margaret Mead established a visual ethnography with their study of "Balinese Character" (1942). Harper advises sociology to "open the eyes of the discipline to a wider and infinitely more interesting perceptual world than a computer screen filled with numbers" (2012, p. 4).

As advances in technological reproduction in the late nineteenth century allowed photography to enter into print media, this went along with a new faith in objectivity. At the time, the photograph was considered the reflection of reality—in contrast to text, in which an author "formed" the events through narrative. This assumption is now outdated—and not only because of the technical possibilities of image manipulation. Every image is made from a particular perspective, since it is people—and not cameras—who take the pictures. An arbitrary component is therefore always manifest (Ball and Smith 2009, p. 305). Photos are "subjectively re-shaped by the photographer" (Baur and Budenz 2017, p. 93). They are not objective representations. On Howard S. Becker's account, the difference between journalistic and sociological photos consists entirely in their context (1995, p. 12): The same photograph can appear in a social science journal or a newspaper. It can be situated within a sociological or a journalistic context. The context determines what sort of image we see.

Such theoretical considerations of images are as relevant for a photograph used in ethnography as for photojournalism. Take for instance the aforementioned crime beat reporter Jacob A. Riis (1997). In the late nineteenth century, he went around the streets of lower Manhattan, where immigration was giving rise to neighborhoods like Little Italy, China Town, and the Jewish Lower East Side. Riis was among the first to use the flash at night in order to show and shed light on the flip side of life— the life of the marginalized. He presented "night-time people in a surreal visual universe" (Harper 2012, p. 24). His photos are hybrids of journalistic and ethnographic photography. The photographer and visual ethnographer Camilo Jose Vergara, who took documentary photos of ghettos in the USA, among other things, operated within a similar tradition (2014).

In the early twentieth century, film was increasingly employed in anthropological fieldwork (Tuma et al. 2013, p. 24 ff.). A classic of ethnographic film released in the early 1920s is *Nanook of the North* by Robert J. Flaherty, who lived for several months with the Inuit and documented their everyday lives. The documentary film demonstrates that the genre is not without dramaturgical elements: The film produces a romanticized image of the Innuit lifeworld with stylistic means and music. Film and photos are—like texts—constructions and not reflections of reality. They are "transformations of lifeworld situations" (Schnettler and Knoblauch 2009, p. 277) and the producers of the visual data are enmeshed in this process.

A person with a camera is not neutral. Their behavior is fundamentally determined by technology (Eberle 2017a, p. 28, 2017b, p. 100 ff.). Photography itself is a physical act, in which the photographer bends, kneels, lies down on the ground, or even climbs up to high places (Eberle 2017b, p. 108). And every shot with the camera is preceded by a selection. "Even the decision as to when the investigation is concluded and the camera unpacked represents a selection—just like the focus and duration of the shooting" (Tuma et al. 2013, p. 12).

In the context of the contingent conditions of the production of visual data, it is also important to consider that people in the field will be conscious of the presence of the researcher's camera and will react to it (Pink 2015, p. 48; Tuma et al. 2013, p. 13). The nature of this reaction depends substantially on how the camera is handled: whether it is mounted on a tripod in the field or whether filming is simply done with a smartphone produces not just a different type of reaction in the field, but also different kinds of aesthetic representations of the course of social activity in the field.

5.18 Factors that Influence Production of Visual Data

Photography can facilitate the first contact in the field: The question of whether one might be allowed to take photographs is—depending on the field—well-suited for establishing contact and possibly conducting a spontaneous interview. In our fieldwork with the disabled in Angola the visibility of the camera often led to the landmine victims posing for the picture. This proved to be fruitful during one excursion to a musseque where the designer Bitten Stetter and the photographer Flurina Rothenberger were also there gathering audiovisual material during a Kuduro production. This was later edited into a video clip, which then became part of the exhibition "Sometimes people in Luanda shine."[10]

Tuma et al. have identified three factors that influence the production of visual data (Tuma et al. 2013, p. 37 ff.):

- *Research situation*

    This dimension relates to the aforementioned dichotomy between natural and artificial situations. Would the situation being filmed be taking place without the presence of the researchers? Do the people in the field know that they are being filmed? Are they reacting to the investigator's camera?

---

[10]The exhibition "Sometimes people in Luanda shine. About landmines, disability and creativity in urban landscapes," curated by Bitten Stetter and Flurina Rothenberger, was shown March 9–16, 2015 in the Zurich Hochschule der Künste. The video "Throbosis," which was edited by the ethnologist Sandra Gysi, can be seen at http://www.bittenstetter.com/sometimes-people-in-luanda-shine/ (accessed 30 June 2019).

- *Operation of the camera*

  How the camera is used is central. Will it be mounted in place to film a particular part of the space over some length of time? Is the researcher filming with a subjective, moving camera, such that the film represents their perspective? Or will film material be included that was produced by the people in the field independently of the investigation? In the last case, the aesthetics with which the people in the field produce their films would also be investigated, among other things.

- *Post-processing*

  Post-processing is relevant for visual data that have been produced independently of the investigation. Here, it is not only the filmed or photographed events, objects, and actions that play a role, but also how these have been edited afterward. This can include cuts, color filters, time-lapse, dubbing, etc. Such stylistic devices make visible the aesthetic specific to a milieu, a group, or a scene.

Tuma et al. define video ethnography as follows: "Researchers go 'into the field' and focus the video camera on everyday situations in which people are engaged in actions and analyze how they are doing it" (Tuma et al. 2013, p. 10). This data—whether still photographs or film—serves primarily as documentation. While field notes are reconstructive, photos and video recordings are *simultaneous* technical recordings of a fluid moment or timespan. In contrast to notes, visual data—in particular moving images with sound—are highly complex and enable microscopic analysis of individual details and sequences of events, which would not be possible with classical reconstructive survey methods (Schnettler and Knoblauch 2009, p. 276).

The production of film has become technologically easier and has a much lower threshold. Whereas entire film and photography crews once went into the field with tripods and technical equipment, operating there as a collective and colonizing the field, today a single researcher with a smartphone can produce video material. Such researchers are more agile—physically and mentally—and more empathetic and less disruptive of a situation, because smartphones are ubiquitous. At the same time, this can lead to the production of an enormous amount of video material, which can in turn make analysis more difficult. The ethnologist Barbara Keifenheim therefore sees something disciplined in working with 16-mm film: one knows that the recording time is limited and the processing costs high, which demands a focused eye when the camera is turned on (2008, p. 278 f.).

5.19 Participant Produced Images

"Participant produced images" (Pink 2013, p. 86 ff.) describes visual data created by the people in the field—for instance, for posting on social media. The resulting images and videos are then "liked," evaluated, and commented on there. Such data are "natural"—produced in the field without the researcher actively eliciting them.

These data can serve as the basis for in-depth interviews or discussions in focus groups. Of course, analog images can function similarly. For instance, in her ethnographic investigations of bullfighting, Sarah Pink has conducted interviews about photographs in clubs for bullfighting aficionados (2013, p. 95 ff.).

Digital photography fundamentally changes image-making practices. In this regard, Nina Baur and Patrick Budenz list the following techniques (2017, p. 77 ff.): *staging and retouching*, *choice of framing*, *focal distance to the object*, *depth of field*, and *coloration*. Eisewicht and Grenz describe digital photography as *interpretative conservation* and identify three levels (2017, p. 121 f.):

- *Camera software for shooting*: Tools to improve image quality, tools that preset certain picture modes, and tools with special trigger mechanisms
- *Camera software for editing existing images*: Editing of existing image data, editing through addition of material and through rearrangement
- *Camera software for managing images*: Sharing, sorting, and backing up photos

The various processing technologies give rise to new aesthetic dimensions that are particularly relevant when analyzing visual data that was produced by participants in the field.

5.20 Digital Ethnography

In the wake of digitization, a flood of new textual and above all visual data has been created. Not only has the quantity of data increased dramatically, but the quality has also fundamentally been altered, which manifests itself in new methods such as *Online Ethnography* (Boellstorff et al. 2012; Hine 2015), *Netnography* (Kozinets 2010, 2019), *Digital Ethnography* (Pink et al. 2016) and *Armchair Anthropology* (Ge 2017), in which visuality must be methodologically taken into account (Gómez Cruz et al. 2017). Every special interest community exchanges experiences through social media. They communicate about diseases, addictions, extreme sports, politics, anxiety, and sexual practices. A distinction should however first be made between "online communities" and "communities online" (Kozinets 2010, p. 63 ff.). Communities online are actually existing communities that have a supplemental platform on the internet. Online communities, on the other hand, are communities that have formed solely on the internet, whose members in most cases never see each other face-to-face.

Similarly to the way the emergence of the novel in the eighteenth century privileged subjectivity and individualization, the internet also gives rise to new forms of visual identity. Codes, symbols, and signs are used as resources in order to express subjective states or desired identities that orient themselves on existing patterns of identity. In this way, digital realities become a site where "expression and perception of the self are pre-structured in a specific way but are also malleable" (Muri 2010, p. 87). Norms are negotiated through likes and comments (Müller 2018). Selfies exhibit a standardized pattern and they objectivize normative patterns of self-representation. These can pertain to the pose, the social constellation (selfies with friends), the facial expression ("duckface"), or even individual body parts ("belfies"). At the same time, however, these normative patterns are continually transformed subjectively. Style and aesthetics are worked out through filters, through which process however adaption and new interpretations repeatedly favor precisely the objectivization (Baur and Budenz 2017, p. 93). In the context of selfies, Neumann-Braun speaks of photographer and feedbacks being "part of a glocal peer review system" (2017, p. 345). Pink notes:

> Moreover, the rapid rise in popularity on the 'selfie' practice of photographing oneself with a smartphone, indicates the closeness that these technologies have to the ways people view and represent their own identities, thus suggesting that the personalization, closeness and affective qualities of the smartphones create potential to similarly create empathetic and corporal connections with audiences through sensory ethnography media. (Pink 2015, p. 165)

Selfies are produced in certain contexts—such as in museums, in front of tourist attractions, at parties, at home in the bathroom, or in bed. The poses are rehearsed and normative. They display a *generalized other* (Mead 2015, p. 152 ff.) and a social *front region* (Goffman 1956, p. 67). A photo that deviates from the norm would not be published; it would damage the image of the depicted person. Which norm applies depends on the social environment. There is great differentiation in this regard. For instance, in the context of mental health, where teens and young adults negotiate psychological suffering and subjective mental sates in digital media, quite particular self-representations are practiced: Young people touch their faces with their hands or show themselves in vulnerable poses in bed, which becomes a symbolic Safe Space (Schmocker 2018, p. 51 ff.).

Kozinets defines netnography (2010) as "participant-observational research based in online fieldwork. It uses computer-mediated communications as a source of data to arrive at the ethnographic understanding and representation of a cultural and communal phenomenon" (2010, p. 50). The specific aspect of his netnography consists in the fact that—just as in ordinary ethnography—the interaction of the researcher with the participants occurs in the field (2010, p. 50). This means that the researcher participates actively in forum discussions, posts images to generate comments, and responds to these: "Online interaction forces the learning of additional codes and norms, abbreviations, emoticons, sets of keystrokes and other technical skills in order to transfer the emotional information vital to social relations" (Kozinets 2010, p. 69). The principle of active participatory observation is translated to digital reality. Further, Kozinets proposes a "blended ethnography," in which online research is combined with research in real-world situations (2010, p. 55 ff.). The process enables identification of the following:

- *Integration vs. Separation of Social Worlds*: What constitutes the similarities and differences in the patterns of behavior in internet and face-to-face situations?
- *Observation vs. Verbalization of Relevant Data*: What it the relationship between observing physical behavior and articulating its description? Are there deviations?

- *Identification vs. Performance of Members*: How relevant are demographic characteristics such as age, ethnicity, gender, etc. of members of a particular community? Or do they distinguish themselves solely through certain contributions or actions?

With *Mediated Sensory Ethnography* (Pink 2015, p. 117 ff.), the action is not reduced to virtual reality; the sensory dimension is also included. The focus is thus on visual, auditory, tactile, and other sensory experiences that occur with digital practices (Pink 2006, p. 44 ff.). For digital technologies continue to appear object-like to us. There is (still) some physical interaction with a device—for instance, a touch screen, a keyboard, a microphone, etc.

5.21 Participatory Action Research

In a certain sense, ethnography is always participatory, since the researcher participates to a greater or lesser extent in the field. Most design processes also have participative elements, given that designers do not just tinker in a lab but rather develop their solutions interactively with particular groups. However, the concept would become diluted if every study and every design were described as participatory. The methods described as participatory in what follows, therefore, are specifically those in which researchers work together with the participants to produce ethnographic data and/or design solutions, or brief them about producing data and solutions themselves. The basic principle is: "Good research is research conducted *with* people rather than *on* people" (Heron and Reason 2006, p. 179).

Participative research and design approaches emerged in Scandinavia in the late 1960s and 1970s (Bjerknes et al. 1987; Blomberg and Karasti 2013, p. 87; Kensing and Greenbaum 2013, p. 27 ff.). "Design Participation" was the theme of the annual conference of the *Design Research Society* in Manchester in 1971 (Robertson and Simonsen 2013, p. 2). In terms of theoretical background, participatory approaches draw on a Marxist-oriented critique of society (Rahman 2008, p. 49) and a critique of positivist sciences (Gergen and Gergen 2008, p. 159). The Marxist idea posits that underprivileged people and societies can improve their situations in collaboration with researchers (Rahman 2008, p. 49). A problem to be solved together serves as the starting point. Robertson and Simonsen define Participatory Design as

> a process of investigating, understanding, reflecting upon, establishing, developing, and supporting mutual learning between multiple participants in collective 'reflection-in-action.' The participants typically undertake the two principal roles of users and designers where the designers strive to learn the realities of the users' situation while the users strive to articulate their desired aims and learn appropriate technological means to obtain them. (Robertson and Simonsen 2013, p. 2)

The participants thus are designers *and* users—and by articulating their concerns and aims they figure out how to achieve the latter. In this process, all the parties involved in the research project should benefit from it: Designers develop design approaches, anthropologists gain insights, and participants solve problems through collaboration. In practice, this means that privileged academics work together with underprivileged people, which requires ethical consideration. Castillo-Burguete et al. describe participation in local communities as a form of *cultural capital*, in Pierre Bourdieu's sense, that must be incorporated and mobilized jointly (2009, p. 532). This does not mean that the communities in question are to be colonized but rather that an exchange of ideas takes place.

5.22 Participatory Photography and Cultural Probes

Participative photography and video means handing out cameras and letting people in the field use them themselves. This approach was employed by Ruth Holliday, who called upon participants to produce "video diaries" (2000). Holliday also explored queer identities this way by asking 15 people from the queer scene to take pictures of their clothing practices at home, going out, and at work (2007, p. 257 ff.). Eric Michaels and Francis Kelly (1984) proceeded similarly when they gave out cameras to Aborigines and had them produce images. In our project in Angola, we gave disposable cameras to students of rehabilitation medicine, who in turn passed these out to physically disabled people so they could take photographs from within their own lifeworlds. The response rate was relatively low, which was in part due to the fact that we did not give out the cameras directly but via a social node. This made the channels of communication significantly more challenging. It was much more productive when we actually included one of these students in the project. Domingos João Pedro Bernardo, who was himself a victim of polio, produced a poem (Bernardo 2016, p. 35) and photos from his lifeworld that were incorporated in our publication (Müller 2016).

Even when researchers are physically absent during the production of the photographs, they are still part of the process through the briefings (Pfadenhauer 2017, p. 136 f.). Such briefings might put the focus on various realms of the everyday world—for instance, things in one's home that are considered beautiful, disruptive, clean, or dirty. The issue here is not just what people will film or consider relevant, but also *how* they will film: that is, how is the camera deployed and moved, what framing is chosen, etc. (Keifenheim 2008, p. 282).

Giaccardi et al. suggest delegating the filming to things and employing them as "co-ethnographers" or "autographers" (2016, p. 235 ff.). In their research project "Thing Tank" they attached small cameras that took photos automatically to three everyday objects—a kettle, a refrigerator, and a tea cup. These "autographers" uncover blind spots, such as the contact or interaction they have with other objects. "A thing perspective opens up possibilities for understanding the limits of human action on time and space and the ways in which non-human things are directly informing and creating the everyday realities in which people live" (Giaccardi et al. 2016, p. 243).

Photovoice was developed by Caroline Wang and Mary Ann Burris (1997). In a study, Wang encouraged women in a rural area in China to take pictures relating to their health situation in their everyday work context. The impetus for the study was the hypothesis that health problems existed there. The procedure had three objectives: First, it aimed to motivate the women to empower themselves to represent and reflect upon their personal and shared strengths and worries. Second, the photos were intended to generate a dialogue about the personal and shared concerns. Third, it sought to reach the level of politics and engage it in dialogue. The method was grounded in the assumption that photos show how we live and how we define ourselves in relation to the world. The methodological approach is described as follows (Wang 1999, p. 187 ff.):

- *Select and recruit a target audience and community leaders*
- *Recruit a group of photovoice participants*
- *Introduce the photovoice methodology to participants and facilitate a group discussion*
- *Obtain informed content*
- *Pose an initial theme for taking pictures*
- *Distribute cameras to participants and review how to use them*
- *Provide time for participants to take pictures*
- *Meet to discuss photographs*
- *Plan with participants a format to share photographs and stories with policy makers or community leaders*

A different direction is taken by the method suggested by Sarah Pink—"Walking with Video" (2007b, 2015, p. 111)—in which the researcher accompanies the participants on walks while simultaneously filming them. This method is based on the assumption that routes and paths do not simply connect start and end points in a functional way but also represent subjective sensory microcosms. By filming directly, the researcher can make reference to the things that are present and make them an immediate subject of the conversation: "Walking with video, I suggest, can generate a more involved approach to the question of how places and identities are constituted" (Pink 2007b, p. 250).

The cultural probes process developed by Bill Gaver in the late 1990s is an extension of the participatory approach (Gaver et al. 1999, 2004; Brandes et al. 2009, p. 168 ff.). The background for it was a study on the elderly in Oslo, Amsterdam, and an area near Pisa. Gaver et al. distributed sets of several postcards to the participants that posed questions about their wishes, everyday worlds, and objects. The sets also contained cards with poetic and sometimes direct questions, such as where participants prefer to meet people, where they are alone, or where they would most like to go but are can't. The participants were given disposable cameras and were asked to photograph where they lived, something they wished for, and something boring. In addition, they received a photo album in which they were supposed to tell their life story in six to ten images. Finally, they were to keep a media diary in which they would record their media consumption—that is, which newspapers they read, which radio programs they heard, and what they watched on television (and with whom they did so) (Gaver et al. 1999, p. 22 ff.). Cultural probes are conceived as an open method that lends itself easily to expansion, supplementation, and alteration (Gaver et al. 2004).

5.23 Photo Elicitation

In "photo elicitation" (Harper 2002, 2012, pp. 155 ff., 81 ff.; Pink 2015, p. 92 ff.) pictures are not simply analyzed by researchers but also function as the basis for interviews with the participants in the field. This method was developed in the 1950s by John Collier (1957, p. 846 ff., 1967, p. 46 ff.). At the time, Collier was conducting interviews with and without photos for a 3-year study on the lifeworlds of workers in Canada. He came to the conclusion that in the interviews with photos, the responses were more precise because the images built a "language bridge" (Collier 1957, p. 858).

The driving assumption here is that the meanings of photographs are not inherent but ascribed (Harper 2002, p. 13; Pink 2013, p. 92). Multiple perspectives on an image open up multiple schemes of interpretation. These interpretations should not be understood as purely subjective processes because categories of cultural signification impact these processes as well. Photo elicitation leads to a new definition of the sociological interview "because it centers an object in a photo that both parties are looking at and trying to make sense of" (Harper 2012, p. 157). As Sarah Pink demonstrates in her empirical investigations of bullfighting in Spain, opponents and aficionados of the practice interpret images differently. In her study, Pink defines three groups that hold diverging positions on bullfighting and female bullfighters: First, bullfighting aficionados who favor female bullfighters; second, bullfighting aficionados who are opposed to female bullfighters; and third, opponents of bullfighting as such (2013, p. 77). Pink conducted interviews focused on images of the bullfighter Cristina Sánchez with people from all three of these groups, which demonstrated that they ascribed varying meanings to the pictures. For instance, if a picture showed Christina Sánchez in a challenging situation, then for the proponents of female bullfighting it was proof that women are capable of mastering it. In contrast, the aficionados opposed to female bullfighters saw in the image a confirmation of their preconceived belief that women are unsuited for it, while the opponents of bullfighting as such saw the superiority of the bull. The interviews that are centered around images thus seek to pluralize perspectives:

> Photo-elicitation relies on the idea of the photograph becoming a visual text through which the subjectivities of researcher and participant intersect. It can evoke memories, knowledge and more in the research participant, which might have otherwise been inaccessible, while simultaneously allowing the researcher to compare her or his subjective interpretation of the image with that of the research participant. (Pink 2015, p. 88)

The image functions as a starting point for seeking out new contexts of meaning and new patterns of interpretation. This can take place in various settings.

Researchers can ask participants to comment on photographs in writing. Photos can serve as the basis for face-to-face interviews, group discussions, and focus groups. In the context of a netnography, photos and videos could be posted online, where they can be commented on, evaluated, and/or altered.

Anna Brake points to several factors that play a relevant role in photo elicitation and are as pertinent to the production of visual materials as to the manner in which the interviews are conducted (2009, p. 376 f.):

- *Photographic material*: This material can come from either the researcher or from the people in the investigated field. There, in turn, it can be produced explicitly for the study or be pre-existing (for instance, family or travel photos, profile pictures from Facebook, Instagram, etc.).
- *Interviews*: The photographic material can be employed quite differently in the interviews. With a structured approach, the sequence, time frame, and questions are defined in advance. With an open approach, respondents can choose the photographs and the duration of the commentary themselves
- *Social constellation*: The inquiry can be conducted in different constellations—in pairs (an interviewer and a respondent) or in larger groups.
- *Media*: The visual materials can be displayed in various media—as prints, on a screen, or projected onto a wall. The medium in which the material is produced can also vary—from photos, sketches, journals, or design tasks to film.
- *Text and visual analysis*: The comments of the respondents are recorded and transcribed and the transcriptions and visual data are interpreted and analyzed, whereby the relative weight given to text and image-based data can vary.

5.24 Interventions

Ethnography in social science research is interested in the natural environment of foreign groups. As already noted, however, researchers also bring forth the world that they observe and identify. In contrast to descriptive ethnography, design intervenes in and alters situations. Design ethnography is based on iterative steps that cycle between description, interpretation, and intervention:

> These include interventionist forms of fieldwork and design that work through iterative cycles of reflection and action, and employ methods and tools such as video feedbacks, scenarios, mock-ups, props, provo- and prototypes, tangible interactions, and various forms of games, performances and enactment. (Otto and Smith 2013, p. 11)

Collaborative approaches such as co-production of a film, joint preparation of a recipe, or participatory design of a prototype are interventions (Pink 2015, p. 7). A design object, after all, does not yet exist during the design process, which is why it cannot be investigated with a conventional ethnographic research approach (Halse 2013, p. 282). The "natural" context in which a new design object will be used cannot be empirically investigated. This is why it is necessary to design prototypes that can be used to intervene in everyday situations. These design interventions can be described broadly as experiments (Hegel et al. 2019), in the sense of open-ended experiments, not those that confirm or refute a hypothesis. Joachim Halse and Laura Boffi speak of "Design Interventions as a Form of Inquiry" and define the method as

> a form of inquiry that is particularly relevant for investigating phenomena that are not very coherent, barely possible, almost unthinkable, and consistently under-specified because they are still in the process of being conceptually and physically articulated. (Halse and Boffi 2016, p. 89)

Fundamental design methods such as prototyping and sketching are used to intervene in order to see lifeworld contexts and segments of reality in a new light. According to Friedrich Stephan, designers take on "the role of creatively destroying certainties and seek occasions for disruptions that call for and enable new adaptations" (2010, p. 86).[11] Gatt and Ingold write that "anthropology-by-means-of-ethnography" is a practice of description while "anthropology-by-means-of-design" in contrast is a practice of correspondence and mediation (2013, p. 144). Barbara Tedlock writes of a development "from Participant Observation to the Observation of Participation" (1991).

5.25 Withdrawing from the Field

Especially during longer and more actively participatory fieldwork, relationships and possibly even friendships between the researcher and the participants develop. There grows a mutual empathy and intimacy. While at the start of the process the researcher may still be an irritant, the participants will have soon become used to him. But every research project must come to a temporal end, at which point the researcher retreats from the field—at least in his role as researcher. If the researcher remains emotionally and socially connected to the people in the investigated lifeworld, this is described as "going native" (Knoblauch 2003, p. 96 ff.). But even where the researcher does not become a "convert" to the group in question, other forms of relationship still arise—for instance, a moral one, as when the researcher has investigated a socially marginalized group and afterwards engages in political activism on their behalf, which may be seen as what César Cisneros Puebla has called "activemia" (2016, p. 173 ff.), a combination of political activism and academic knowledge. Another ethically important point, of course, comes when the researcher publishes about the studied group. In this regard, Roland Girtler recommends sharing the data and texts with the participants prior to publication

---

[11]Noteworthy in that regard is the work of Andrea Staudacher, who experiments in her Future Food Lab with the cultural acceptance of insects and in-vitro meat (2015). The aim is to show that social norms surrounding food can be reconsidered and reflected upon and new patterns of consumption can be explored. Staudacher wants to create awareness for the nutritional possibilities of the future. https://www.futurefoodlab.ch. accessed 17 August 2019.

and discussing them together (2001, p. 128 ff.). The ethical questions raised by the retreat from the field will be dealt with in the next chapter.

5.26 Ethics

In contrast to morality, which is based on socially accepted values and norms, ethics is reflective. It begins at the point where moral concepts are questioned and considered (Luhmann 2008, p. 372). Ethnographic fieldwork gives rise to numerous ethical concerns (Roth and von Unger 2018) that often have to do with various kinds of disparities between the researcher and the participants in the field. While such disparities do not speak against the project at all, still they need to be taken into consideration. The American Anthropological Association advocates the following seven points on the question of ethics:[12]

1. Do No Harm
2. Be Open and Honest Regarding Your Work
3. Obtain Informed Consent and Necessary Permissions
4. Weigh Competing Ethical Obligations Due Collaborators and Affected Parties
5. Make Your Results Accessible
6. Protect and Preserve Your Records
7. Maintain Respectful and Ethical Professional Relationships

Concretely, the ethical questions concern primarily personal rights. In contrast to quantitative research, where reports are based mainly on statistical data, ethnography sketches out people's lifeworlds. Participants tell their life stories, offer a view into their everyday worlds, and perhaps reveal intimate and embarrassing details. If this information is published, it can harm those involved, which must absolutely be avoided. The issues that are associated with this must be weighed carefully, especially in research with children or people will impaired judgment. Consent must be obtained from parents or appropriate authorities.

An important point concerns the way in which research data is made available to the public. In the case of textual data, there are varying degrees of anonymization. But visual data is different (Pink 2015, p. 67 ff.; Schnettler and Knoblauch 2009, p. 279; Tuma et al. 2013, p. 67 f.): Since people are photographed or filmed, they are identifiable. They should therefore be informed of any publication and give their consent. Sarah Pink recommends involving the people from the investigated lifeworlds in the research process rather than defining them as objects (2015, p. 68).

---

[12] http://ethics.americananthro.org/category/statement/ (accessed 11 July 2019).

References

Adams, R. (1975). *Interracial marriage in Hawaii.* New York: AMS Press.
Anderson, N. (1998). *On hobos and homelessness. Heritage of sociology.* Chicago: University of Chicago Press.
Appadurai, A. (1986). *The social life of things: Commodities in cultural perspective.* Cambridge: Cambridge University Press.
Arantes, L. M., & Rieger, E. (2014). Ethnographien der Sinne. In *Wahrnehmung und Methode in empirisch kulturwissenschaftlichen Forschungen* [Ethnographies of the senses: Perception and method in empirical cultural studies]. Bielefeld: Transcript.
Ball, M., & Smith, G. (2009). Technologies of realism. In P. Atkinson, A. Coffey, S. Delamont, J. Lofland, & L. Lofland (Eds.), *Handbook of ethnography* (pp. 302–319). London: Sage.
Bannon, L. G., & Bødker, S. (1991). Beyond the interface: Encountering artifacts in use. In J. M. Carroll (Ed.), *Designing interaction: Psychology at the human-computer interface* (pp. 227–253). Cambridge: Cambridge University Press.
Bateson, G., & Mead, M. (1942). *Balinese character.* New York: New York Academy of Sciences.
Baur, N., & Budenz, P. (2017). Fotografisches Handeln. Subjektive Überformung von fotografischen Repräsentationen von Wirklichkeit [Photographic action: Subjective transformation of photographic representations of reality]. In T. S. Eberle (Ed.), *Fotografie und Gesellschaft. Phänomenologische und wissenssoziologische Perspektiven* [Photography and society: Phenomenological and sociological perspectives] (pp. 73–96). Bielefeld: Transcript.
Becker, H. S. (1995). Visual sociology, documentary photography, and photojournalism: It's (almost) all a matter of context. *Visual Sociology, 10*(1–2), 5–14.
Bell, J. A., & Kuipers, J. C. (2018). *Linguistic and material intimacies of cell phones.* New York: Routledge.
Bell, G., Blythe, M., & Sengers, P. (2006). Making by making strange. *ACM ToCHI, 12*(2), 149–173.
Berger, P. L., & Luckmann, T. (1967). *The social construction of reality: A treatise in the sociology of knowledge.* New York: Anchor.
Bernardo, D. J. P. (2016). An mein Luanda [To my Luanda]. In F. Müller (Ed.), *Mit Behinderung in Angola leben. Eine ethnografische Spurensuche in einer von Tretminen verletzten Gesellschaft* [Living with disabilities in Angola: An ethnographic search for clues in a society injured by mines] (p. 35). Bielefeld: Transcript.
Bjerknes, G., Ehn, P., & Kyng, M. (1987). *Computers and democracy: A Scandinavian challenge.* Aldershot: Avebury.
Blomberg, J., & Karasti, H. (2013). Ethnography: Positioning ethnography within participatory design. In J. Simonsen & T. Robertson (Eds.), *International handbook of participatory design* (pp. 86–116). London: Routledge.
Blomberg, J., Giacomi, J., Mosher, A., & Swenton-Wall, P. (1993). Ethnographic field methods and their relation to design. In D. Schuler & A. Namioka (Eds.), *Participatory design: Principles and practices* (pp. 123–155). Hillsdale, NJ: Lawrence Erlbaum.
Bly, N. (2009). *Ten days in a mad-house.* Rockville, MD: Wildside Press.
Boehm, G. (1994). Jenseits der Sprache? Anmerkungen zur Logik der Bilder [Beyond language? Comments on the logic of pictures]. In C. Maar & H. Burda (Eds.), *Iconic Turn. Die neue Macht der Bilder* [Iconic turn: The new power of images] (pp. 28–43). Cologne: Dumont.
Boellstorff, T., Nardie, B., Pearce, C., & Taylor, T. L. (2012). *Ethnography and virtual worlds: A handbook of method.* Oxford: Princeton University Press.
Böhme, H. (2012). *Fetischismus und Kultur. Eine andere Theorie der Moderne* [Fetishism and culture: Another theory of modernity]. Reinbek: Rowohlt.
Brake, A. (2009). Photobasierte Befragung [Photo-based survey]. In S. Kühl, P. Strodtholz, & A. Taffertshofer (Ed.), *Handbuch Methoden der Organisationsforschung. Quantitative und qualitative Methoden* [Handbook of methods of organizational research. Quantitative and qualitative methods] (pp. 369–388). Wiesbaden: Springer VS.

References

Brandes, U., Erlhoff, M., & Schemmann, N. (2009). *Designtheorie und Designforschung* [Design theory and design research]. Paderborn: Fink.

Bratteteig, T., Bødker, K., Dittrich, Y., Morgensen, P. H., & Simonsen, J. (2013). Methods: Organising principles and general guidelines for participatory design projects. In J. Simonsen & T. Robertson (Eds.), *International handbook of participatory design* (pp. 117–144). London: Routledge.

Byrne, B. (2012). Qualitative interviewing. In C. Seale (Ed.), *Researching society and culture* (pp. 206–226). London: Sage.

Campbell, C. (1998). Consumption and the rhetorics of need and want. *Journal of Design History, 11*, 235–246.

Castillo-Burguete, M. T., Viga de Alva, M. D., & Dickinson, F. (2009). Changing the culture of dependency to allow successful outcomes in participatory research: Fourteen years of experience in Yucatan, Mexico. In P. Reason & H. Bradbury (Eds.), *Handbook of action research: Participative inquiry and practice* (pp. 522–533). London: Sage.

Charmaz, K., & Mitchell, R. G. (2009). Grounded theory in ethnography. In P. Atkinson, A. Coffey, S. Delamont, J. Lofland, & L. Lofland (Eds.), *Handbook of ethnography* (pp. 160–174). London: Sage.

Cisneros Puebla, C. A. (2016). Sometimes it is only madness that makes us what we are. *International Review of Qualitative Research, 9*(2), 173–177.

Clarke, A. J. (2016). The new ethnographers 1968–1974: Towards a critical historiography of design anthropology. In R. C. Smith, K. T. Vangkilde, M. G. Kjærsgaard, T. Otto, J. Halse, & T. Binder (Eds.), *Design anthropological futures* (pp. 71–85). London: Bloomsbury.

Clarke, A. J. (2017). *Design anthropology: Object cultures in transition*. London: Bloomsbury.

Classen, C. (2005). *The book of touch*. Oxford: Berg.

Coffey, A. (1999). *The ethnographic self: Fieldwork and the representation of identity*. London: Sage.

Collier, J. (1957). Photography in anthropology: A report on two experiments. *American Anthropologist, 59*, 843–859.

Collier, J. (1967). *Visual anthropology: Photography as a research method*. New York: Holt, Rinehard and Winston.

Crabtree, A., Rodden, R., Tolmie, P., & Button, G. (2009). Ethnography considered harmful. In: *The status of ethnography in system design* (pp. 879–888). Boston: Association for Computing Machinery (ACM).

Crabtree, A., Roucefield, M., & Tolmie, P. (2012). *Doing design ethnography*. London: Springer.

Cranz, G. (2016). *Ethngraphy for designers*. New York: Routledge.

Cross, N. (2007). From a design science to a design discipline: Understanding designerly ways of knowing and thinking. In R. Michel (Ed.), *Design research now* (pp. 41–54). Basel: Birkhauser.

Cushing, F. H. (1988). *The mythic world of the Zuni*. Albuquerque: University of New Mexico Press.

Deegan, M. J. (2009). The Chicago school of ethnography. In P. Atkinson, A. Coffey, S. Delamont, J. Lofland, & L. Lofland (Eds.), *Handbook of ethno-graphy* (pp. 11–25). Los Angeles: Sage.

Dellwing, M., & Prus, R. (2012). *Einführung in die interaktionistische Ethnografie. Soziologie im Außendienst* [Introduction to interactionist ethnography: Sociology in the field]. Wiesbaden: Springer VS.

Donovan, F. R. (1988). *The saleslady*. Chicago: University of Chicago Press.

Douglas, M. (1966). *Purity and danger: An analysis of the concept of pollution and taboo*. New York: Routledge.

Douglas, M. (2011). *In the active voice*. London: Routledge and Kegan Paul.

Douglas, M., & Isherwood, B. (1978). *The world of goods: Towards an anthropology of consumption*. New York: Penguin Books.

Eberle, T. S. (2017a). Fotografie und Gesellschaft. Theoretische Rahmung [Photography and society: Theoretical framing]. In T. S. Eberle (Ed.), *Fotografie und Gesellschaft. Phänomenologische und wissenssoziologische Perspektiven* [Photography and society: Phenomenological and sociological perspectives] (pp. 11–70). Bielefeld: Transcript.

Eberle, T. S. (2017b). Der Akt des Fotografierens. Eine phänomenologische und autoethnografische Analyse [The act of taking pictures: A phenomenological and auto-ethnographic analysis]. In T. S. Eberle (Ed.), *Fotografie und Gesellschaft. Phänomenologische und wissenssoziologische Perspektiven* [Photography and society: Phenomenological and sociological perspectives] (pp. 97–116). Bielefeld: Transcript.

Eisewicht, P., & Grenz, T. (2017). Zur Veralltäglichung interpretativer Konservierung [On the everyday use of interpretive conservation]. In T. S. Eberle (Ed.), *Fotografie und Gesellschaft. Phänomenologische und wissenssoziologische Perspektiven* [Photography and society: Phenomenological and sociological perspectives] (pp. 117–132). Bielefeld: Transcript.

Emerson, R. M., Fretz, R. I., & Shaw, L. L. (1995). *Writing ethnographic fieldnotes*. Chicago: University of Chicago Press.

Feyerabend, P. (2010). *Against methods*. New York: Verso.

Fleck, L. (1986). To look, to see, to know. In R. S. Cohen & T. Schnelle (Eds.), *Cognition and fact: Materials on Ludwik Fleck*. Dordrecht: Springer. https://doi.org/10.1007/978-94-009-4498-5.

Flick, U. (2014). *An introduction to qualitative research*. London: Sage.

Gatt, C., & Ingold, T. (2013). From description to correspondence: Anthropology in real time. In W. Gunn, T. Otto, & R. C. Smith (Eds.), *Design anthropology: Theory and practice* (pp. 139–159). London: Bloomsbury.

Gaver, B., Dunne, T., & Pacenti, E. (1999). Cultural probes. *Interactions, 1*, 21–29.

Gaver, W. G., Boucher, A., Penington, S., & Walker, B. (2004). Cultural probes and the value of uncertainty. *Interactions, 11*(5), 53–56.

Ge, Z. (2017). Armchair anthropology. In S. Pink (Ed.), *The future of digital ethnography* (pp. 18–19). Melbourne: RMIT University.

Geertz, C. (1999). "From the native's point of view": On the nature of anthropological understanding. In R. T. McCutcheon (Ed.), *The insider/outsider problem in the study of religion* (pp. 50–63). New York: Cassell.

Gergen, K. J., & Gergen, M. M. (2008). Social construction and research as action. In P. Reason & H. Bradbury (Eds.), *Handbook of action research: Participative inquiry and practice* (pp. 159–171). London: Sage.

Geurts, K. L. (2002). On rocks, walks, and walks in West African culture: Cultural categories and anthropology of the senses. *Ethos, 30*(3), 178–198.

Giaccardi, E., Speed, C., Cila, N., & Caldwell, M. L. (2016). Things as co-ethnographers: Implications of a thing perspective for design and anthropology. In R. C. Smith, K. T. Vangkilde, M. G. Kjærsgaard, T. Otto, J. Halse, & T. Binder (Eds.), *Design anthropological futures* (pp. 235–248). London: Bloomsbury.

Girtler, R. (2001). *Methoden der Feldforschung* [Field research methods]. Cologne: Böhlau.

Goffman, E. (1956). *The presentation of self in everyday life*. Edinburgh: University of Edinburgh.

Goffman, E. (1961). On the characteristics of total institutions: The inmate world. In D. R. Cressey (Ed.), *The prison: Studies in institutional organization and change* (pp. 15–67). New York: Holt, Rinehart and Winston.

Goffman, E. (1989). On fieldwork. *Journal of Contemporary Ethnography, 18*, 123–132.

Goffman, E. (2010). *Relations in public: Microstudies of the public order*. New Brunswick: Transaction.

Gómez Cruz, E., Sumartojo, S., & Pink, S. (2017). *Refiguring techniques in digital visual research*. Hampshire: Palgrave Macmillan.

Gould, J. D., & Lewis, C. (1985). Designing for usability: Key principles and what designers thank. *Communications of the ACM, 28*(3), 300–311.

Habermas, T. (1999). *Geliebte Objekte: Symbole und Instrumente der Identitätsbildung* [Beloved objects: Symbols and instruments of identity formation]. Berlin: Suhrkamp.

Hahn, A. (1995). Identität und Biografie [Identity and biography]. In M. Wohlrab-Sahr (Ed.), *Biographie und Religion* [Biography and religion] (pp. 127–151). Main: Campus.

Hahn, H. P. (2014), *Materielle Kultur. Eine Einführung* [Material culture: An introduction]. Berlin: Dietrich Reimer.

Hahn, H. P. (2015). *Vom Eigensinn der Dinge: Für eine neue Perspektive auf die Welt des Materiellen* [On the stubbornness of things: For a new perspective on the world of the material]. Berlin: Neofelis Verlag.

Hahn, H. P., & Schmitz, G. (2018). *Market as place and space of economic exchange: Perspectives from archaeology and anthropology*. Oxford: Oxford Books.

Halse, J. (2013). Ethnographies of the possible. In W. Gunn, T. Otto, & R. C. Smith (Eds.), *Design anthropology: Theory and practice* (pp. 180–196). London: Bloomsbury.

Halse, J., & Boffi, L. (2016). Design interventions as a form of inquiry. In R. C. Smith, K. T. Vangkilde, M. G. Kjærsgaard, T. Otto, J. Halse, & T. Binder (Eds.), *Design anthropological futures* (pp. 89–103). London: Bloomsbury.

Harper, D. (2002). Talking about pictures: A case for photo-elicitation. *Visual Studies, 17*(1), 13–26.

Harper, D. (2012). *Visual sociology*. New York: Routledge.

Hegel, C., Cantarella, L., & Marcus, G. E. (2019). *Ethnography by design: Scenographic experiments in fieldwork*. New York: Bloomsbury Academic.

Hermanns, H. (2008). Interviewen als Tätigkeit [Interviewing as an activity]. In U. Flick, E. von Kardorff, & I. Steinke (Eds.), *Qualitative Forschung. Ein Handbuch* [Qualitative research: A handbook] (pp. 360–368). Reinbek: Rowohlt.

Heron, J., & Reason, P. (2006). The practice of co-operative inquiry: Research "with" rather than "on" people. In P. Reason & H. Bradbury (Eds.), *Handbook of action research: Participative inquiry and practice* (pp. 179–188). London: Sage.

Hine, C. (2015). *Ethnography for the internet: Embedded, embodied and everyday*. New York: Bloomsbury.

Holaschke, L. (2016). *Lipstick Tehran*. Master's thesis. Zurich University of the Arts, Zurich.

Holliday, R. (2000). We've been framed: Visualizing methodology. *Sociological Review, 48*(4), 503–521. https://doi.org/10.1111/1467-954X.00230.

Holliday, R. (2007). Performances, confessions, and identities. Using video diaries to research sexualities. In G. C. Stanczak (Ed.), *Visual Research Methods. Image, Society, and Representation* (pp. 255–305). London: Sage.

Honer, A. (2011). *Kleine Leiblichkeiten. Erkundungen in Lebenswelten* [Small corporealities: Explorations in living environments]. Wiesbaden: Springer VS.

Howes, D. (1991). *The varieties of sensory experience: A sourcebook in the anthropology of the senses*. Toronto: University of Toronto Press.

Hughes, J., King, V., Rodden, T., & Andersen, H. (1994). Moving out of the control room: Ethnography in system design. In R. Futura & C. Neuwirth (Eds.), *Transcending boundaries: Proceedings of the conference on computer supported cooperative work* (pp. 429–439). New York: ACM.

Hughes, J., King, V., Rodden, T., & Anderson, H. (1995). The role of ethnography in interactive system design. *Interactions, 2*(2), 57–65.

Ictech, B. (2019). Smartphones and face-to-face interaction: Digital cross-talk during encounters in everyday life. *Symbolic Interaction, 42*(1), 27–45.

Jotzu, P. (2018). *Smell forward*. Master's thesis. Zurich University of the Arts, Zurich.

James, F. (2016). 'Sketch and talk': An ethnographic design method opening closed institutions. In C. Kung, E. Lam, & Y. Lee (Eds.), *Open desing for everything* (p. 163). Aalto (Finnland): Cumulus International Association of Universities and Colleges of Art, Design and Media.

Katz, J. (2019). On becoming an ethnographer. *Contemporary Ethnography, 48*(1), 16–50. https://doi.org/10.1177/0891241618777801.

Keifenheim, B. (2008). Der Einsatz von Film und Video [The use of film and video]. In B. Beer (Ed.), *Methoden ethnologischer Feldforschung* [Methods of ethnological field research] (pp. 277–291). Berlin: Dietrich Reimer.

Kensing, F., & Greenbaum, J. (2013). Heritage. Having a say. In J. Simonsen & T. Robertson (Eds.), *International handbook of participatory design* (pp. 21–36). New York: Routledge.

Kjærsgaard, M. G., Halse, J., Smith, R. C., Vangkilde, K. T., Binder, T., & Otto, T. (2016). Introduction: Design anthropological futures. In R. C. Smith, K. T. Vangkilde, M. G. Kjærsgaard, T. Otto, J. Halse, & T. Binder (Eds.), *Design anthropological futures* (pp. 1–16). London: Bloomsbury.

Knoblauch, H. (2001). Fokussierte Ethnographie [Focused ethnography]. *Sozialer Sinn* [Social sense], *1*, 123–141.

Knoblauch, H. (2003). *Qualitative Religionsforschung* [Qualitative research on religion]. Paderborn: Schöningh.

Knoblauch, H. (2006). Videography: Focused ethnography and video analysis. In H. Knoblauch, B. Schnettler, J. Raab, & H. G. Soeffner (Eds.), *Video analysis: Methodology and methods. Qualitative audiovisual data analysis in sociology* (pp. 35–50). Main: Peter Lang.

Kozinets, R. V. (2010). *Netnography: Doing ethnographic research online*. London: Sage.

Kozinets, R. V. (2019). *Netnography: The essential guide to qualitative social media research*. London: Sage.

Kusenbach, M. (2008). Mitgehen als Methode: Der "Go-Along" in der phänomenologischen Forschungspraxis [Going along as a method: The 'go-along' in phenomenological research practice]. In J. Raab, M. Pfadenhauer, P. Stegmaier, J. Dreher, & B. Schnettler (Eds.), *Phänomenologie und Soziologie. Theoretische Positionen, aktuelle Problemfelder und empirische Umsetzungen* [Phenomenology and sociology: Theoretical positions, current problem areas and empirical implementations] (pp. 349–358). Wiesbaden: Springer VS.

Latour, B. (2002). *Die Hoffnung der Pandora* [Pandora's hope]. Main: Suhrkamp.

Lee, J., & Ingold, T. (2006). Fieldwork on foot: Perceiving, routing, socializing. In S. Coleman & P. Collins (Eds.), *Locating the field: Space, place and context in anthropology* (pp. 67–85). Oxford: Berg.

Liebold, R., & Trinczek, R. (2009). Experteninterview [Expert interview]. In S. Kühl (Ed.), *Handbuch Methoden der Organisationsforschung. Quantitative und qualitative Methoden* [Handbook of methods of organizational research: Quantitative and qualitative methods] (pp. 32–56). Wiesbaden: Springer VS.

Lindner, R. (2007). *Die Entdeckung der Stadtkultur. Soziologie aus der Erfahrung der Reportage* [The discovery of urban culture. Sociology derived from the experience of reporting]. Main: Campus.

Low, K. E. Y. (2005). Ruminations on smell as a sociocultural phenomenon. *Current Sociology, 53*, 397–417.

Lueger, M. (2000). *Grundlagen qualitativer Feldforschung* [Foundations of qualitative field research]. Vienna: Vienna University.

Lueger, M., & Froschauer, U. (2018). *Artefaktanalyse. Grundlage und Verfahren* [Artifact analysis: Foundations and procedures]. Wiesbaden: Springer VS.

Luhmann, N. (2008). *Die Moral der Gesellschaft* [The morality of society]. Main: Suhrkamp.

Maeder, C. (1995). *In totaler Gesellschaft. Eine ethnografische Untersuchung zum offenen Strafvollzug* [In total society: An ethnographic investigation into the open prison system]. Bamberg: Difo.

Malinowski, B. (1932). *Argonauts of the Western Pacific*. London: George Routledge & Sons.

Marcus, G. E. (1995). Ethnography in/on the world system: The emergence of multi-sited ethnography. *Annual Review of Anthropology, 24*, 95–117.

Mareis, C., Held, M., & Joost, G. (2013). *Wer gestaltet die Gestaltung? Theorie, Praxis und Geschichte des partizipatorischen Designs* [Who designs the design? Theory, practice and history of participatory design]. Bielefeld: Transcript.

Maturana, H. R., & Varela, F. J. (2003). *El árbol del conocimiento. Las bases biológicas del entendimiento humano* [The tree of knowledge: The biological basis of human understanding]. Buenos Aires: Lumen.

Mead, G. H. (2015). *Mind, self & society*. Chicago: University of Chicago Press.

Merton, R. K. (1987). The focused interview and focus groups: Continuities and discontinuities. *Public Opinion Quarterly, 51*, 550–556.

Michaels, E., & Kelly, F. (1984). The social organisation of an Aboriginal video workplace. *Australian Aboriginal Studies, 84*, 26–34.
Milev, Y. (2015). Gestalten [Shape]. In J. Badura, S. Dubach, A. Haarmann, D. Mersch, A. Rey, C. Schenker & G. T. Pérez (Eds.), *Künstlerische Forschung. Ein Handbuch* [Artistic research: A handbook] (pp. 143–146). Zurich: Diaphanes.
Miller, D. (2008). *The comfort of things*. Cambridge: Polity Press.
Miller, D. (2009a). *Stuff*. Cambridge, MA: Polity Press.
Miller, D. (2009b). Why clothing is not superficial. In D. Miller (Ed.), *Stuff* (pp. 13–41). Cambridge: Polity Press.
Miller, D. (2011). The poverty of morality. *Journal of Consumer Culture, 1*(2), 225–243. https://doi.org/10.1177/146954050100100210.
Miller, D. (2013). Consumption. In C. Tilley, W. Keane, S. Kuechler-Fogden, M. Rowlands, & P. Spyer (Eds.), *Handbook of material culture* (pp. 341–354). London: Sage.
Moorman, M. J. (2008). *Intonations: A social history of music and nation in Luanda, Angola, from 1945 to recent times*. Athens, OH: Ohio University Press.
Müller, F. (2015). *Selbsttransformation und charismatisch evangelikale Identität. Eine vergleichende ethnosemantische Lebenswelt-Analyse* [Self-transformation and charismatic evangelical identity: A comparative ethnosemantic lifeworld analysis]. Wiesbaden: Springer VS.
Müller, F. (2016). *Mit Behinderung in Angola leben. Eine ethnografische Spurensuche in einer von Tretminen verletzten Gesellschaft* [Living with disabilities in Angola: An ethnographic search for clues in a society injured by mines]. Bielefeld: Transcript.
Müller, F. (2018). Das ästhetische Echo des Sozialen. Identitätskonstruktion durch Mikropraktiken und kulturelle Ressourcen [The aesthetic echo of the social: Identity construction through micropractices and cultural resources]. In G. Muri, D. Späti, P. Klaus, & F. Müller (Eds.), *Eventisierung der Stadt* [Eventization of the city] (pp. 183–191). Berlin: Jovis.
Müller, F. (2019). Pluralizing perspectives on material culture: An essay on design ethnography and the world of things. *DIS Journal 4*(3), 41–62. Mexico City: Diseño y Cultura [Design and Culture], Ibero-American University. Retrieved August 17, 2019, from http://disjournal.ibero.mx/index.php/DISJournal/issue/view/5/DIS_3_4?fbclid=IwAR21lhtn0RaoKQx-y8pUiC9fudZFe3v4xQlcukUH8CY3Wd7rBbPm-EbcwHQ
Muri, G. (2010). "Wer bin ich?"—Identitäten und Ressourcen ["Who am I?"—Identities and resources]. In C. Ritter, G. Muri, & B. Rogger (Eds.), *Magische Ambivalenz. Visualität und Identität im transkulturellen Raum* [Magical ambivalence: Visuality and identity in transcultural space] (pp. 78–96). Zurich: Diaphanes.
Murphy, K. M., & Marcus, G. E. (2013). Epilogue: Ethnography and design, ethnography in design ... ethnography by design. In W. Gunn, T. Otto, & R. C. Smith (Eds.), *Design anthropology: Theory and practice* (pp. 251–268). London: Bloomsbury.
Nardi, B. A. (1993). *A small matter of programming: Perspectives on end user computing*. Cambridge, MA: MIT Press.
Neumann-Braun, K. (2017). Selfies. Oder: kein fotografisches Selbstportrait ohne den Anderen [Selfies. Or. No photographic self-portrait without the other]. In T. S. Eberle (Ed.), *Fotografie und Gesellschaft. Phänomenologische und wissenssoziologische Perspektiven* [Photography and society: Phenomenological and sociological perspectives] (pp. 343–348). Bielefeld: Transcript.
Nova, N. (2014). *Beyond design ethnography: How designers practice ethnographic research*. Geneva: SHS & HEAD.
O'Neill, M., & Hubbard, P. (2010). Walking, sensing, belonging: Ethno-mimesis as performative praxis. *Visual Studies, 25*(1), 46–58. https://doi.org/10.1080/14725861003606878.
Otto, T., & Smith, R. C. (2013). Design anthropology: A distinct style of knowing. In W. Gunn, T. Otto, & R. C. Smith (Eds.), *Design anthropology: Theory and practice* (pp. 1–29). London: Bloomsbury.

Park, R. E., & Burgess, E. W. (1967). *The city: Suggestions for investigation of human behavior in the urban environment.* Chicago: University of Chicago Press.
Pfadenhauer, M. (2002). Auf gleicher Augenhöhe reden. Das Experteninterview: Ein Gespräch zwischen Experte und Quasi-Experte [Speaking at the same eye level. The expert interview: A conversation between an expert and a quasi-expert]. In A. Bogner, B. Littig, & W. Menz (Eds.), *Das Experteninterview. Theorie, Methode, Anwendung* [The expert interview: Theory, method, application] (pp. 113–130). Wiesbaden: Springer VS.
Pfadenhauer, M. (2017). Fotografieren (lassen) in der lebensweltlichen Ethnographie [(Allowing) photography in the ethnography of everyday lifeworlds]. In T. S. Eberle (Ed.), *Fotografie und Gesellschaft. Phänomenologische und wissenssoziologische Perspektiven* [Photography and society: Phenomenological and sociological perspectives] (pp. 133–145). Bielefeld: Transcript.
Pink, S. (2006). *The future of visual anthropology: Engaging the senses.* London: Routledge.
Pink, S. (2007a). *Visual interventions: Applied visual anthropology.* New York: Berghahn.
Pink, S. (2007b). Walking with video. *Visual Studies, 22*(3), 240–252. https://doi.org/10.1080/14725860701657142.
Pink, S. (2011). A multisensory approach to visual methods. In E. Margolis & L. Pauwels (Eds.), *The SAGE handbook of visual research methods* (pp. 601–614). London: Sage.
Pink, S. (2013). *Doing visual ethnography.* London: Sage.
Pink, S. (2014). Digital-Visual-Sensory-Design anthropology: Ethnography, imagination and intervention. *Arts and Humanities in Higher Education, 13*(4), 412–427.
Pink, S. (2015). *Doing sensory ethnography.* London: Sage.
Pink, S., Heather, H., Postill, J., Hjorth, L., Lewis, T., & Tacchi, J. (2016). *Digital ethnography: Principles and practice.* London: Sage.
Prus, R. (1996). *Symbolic interaction and ethnographic research: Intersubjectivity and the study of human lives experience.* Albany, NY: State University of New York Press.
Prus, R. (1997). *Subcultural mosaic and intersubjective realities: An ethnographic research agenda for pragmatizing the social sciences.* Albany, NY: State University of New York Press.
Rahman, A. (2008). Some trends in the praxis of participatory action research. In P. Reason & H. Bradbury (Eds.), *The SAGE handbook of action research: Participative inquiry and practice* (pp. 49–62). London: Sage.
Reason, P. (2004). Critical design ethnography as action research. *Anthropology and Education Quarterly, 35*(2), 269–276. Retrieved August 17, 2019, from https://www.jstor.org/stable/3651406
Reason, P., & Bradbury, H. (2008). *The SAGE handbook of action research: Participative inquiry and practice.* London: Sage.
Reckless, W. (1969). *Vice in Chicago.* Montclair, NJ: Patterson Smith.
Reimers, I. (2014). Ess-Settings als Versammlungen der Sinne [Dining settings as assemblies of the senses]. In L. M. Arantes & E. Rieger (Eds.), *Ethnographien der Sinne. Wahrnehmung und Methode in empirisch kulturwissenschaftlichen Forschungen* [Ethnographies of the senses: Perception and method in empirical cultural studies] (pp. 75–90). Bielefeld: Transcript.
Riis, J. A. (1997). *How the other half lives.* New York: Penguin.
Robertson, T., & Simonsen, J. (2013). Participatory design: An introduction. In T. Robertson & J. Simonsen (Eds.), *International handbook of participatory design* (pp. 1–17). London: Routledge.
Roth, W. M., & von Unger, H. (2018). Current perspectives on research ethics in qualitative research. *FQS Forum Qualitative Social Research, 19*(3). Retrieved August 17, 2019, from http://www.qualitative-research.net/index.php/fqs/article/view/3155
Salvador, T., Bell, G., & Anderson, K. (1999). Design ethnography. *Design Management Journal, 10*(4), 35–41. https://doi.org/10.1111/j.1948-7169.1999.tb00274.x.
Schmocker, A. (2018). *Sick style: The new codes of sadness.* Master's thesis. Zurich: Zurich University of the Arts.

References

Schnettler, B., & Knoblauch, H. (2009). Videoanalyse [Video analysis]. In S. Kühl, P. Strodtholz, & A. Taffertshofer (Eds.), *Handbuch Methoden der Organisationsforschung. Quantitative und qualitative Methoden* [Handbook of methods of organizational research: Quantitative and qualitative methods] (pp. 272–297). Wiesbaden: Springer VS.

Schnettler, B., & Raab, J. (2012). *Video analysis: Methodology and methods: Qualitative audiovisual data analysis in sociology*. Main: Peter Lang.

Schön, D. A. (1983). *The reflexive practitioner: How professionals think in action*. New York: Basic Books.

Schütze, F. (1983). Biografieforschung und narratives Interview [Biography research and narrative interview]. *Neue Praxis. Kritische Zeitschrift für Sozialarbeit und Sozialpädagogik* [New practice: Critical journal for social work and social education] *13*, 283–293. Retrieved August 17, 2019, from https://www.ssoar.info/ssoar/bitstream/handle/document/5314/ssoar-np-1983-3-schutze-biographieforschung_und_narratives_interview.pdf

Shapiro, D. (1994). The limits of ethnography: Combining social sciences for CSCW. In *CSCW' 94 Proceedings on the Conference on Computer Supported Cooperative Work* (pp. 417–428). Chapel Hill, NC: ACM Press. https://doi.org/10.1145/192844.193064.

Sierach, B. (2016). *Intercultural Link. Über die Rolle der Designer/innen in sozialen Projekten* [Intercultural link: On the role of the designer in social projects]. Master's thesis. Zurich: Zurich University of the Arts.

Spradley, J. P. (1979). *The ethnographic interview*. Belmont, CA: Wadsworth.

Spradley, J. P. (1980). *Participant observation*. Belmont, CA: Wadsworth.

Spradley, J. P. (1999). *You owe yourself a drunk: An ethnography of urban nomads*. Longgrove, IL: Waveland Press.

Spradley, J. P., & Mann, B. J. (1975). *The cocktail waitress*. New York: McGraw-Hill.

Spradley, J. P., & Spradley, T. S. (1985). *Deaf like me*. Washington, DC: Gallaudet University Press.

Staudacher, A. (2015). *MMH or HMM. Meinungsbildung durch Ereignisdesign* [Formation of opinion through event design]. Master's thesis. Zurich: Zurich University of the Arts.

Stephan, P. F. (2010). Wissen und Nicht-Wissen im Entwurf [Knowing and not knowing in design]. In C. Mareis, G. Joost, & K. Kimpel (Eds.), *Entwerfen—Wissen—Produzieren. Designforschung im Anwendungskontext* [Design—Knowledge—Production: Design research in an application context] (pp. 81–99). Bielefeld: Transcript.

Stetter, B. (2016). Lange Fingernägel [Long fingernails]. In F. Müller (Ed.), *Mit Behinderung in Angola leben. Eine ethnografische Spurensuche in einer von Tretminen verletzten Gesellschaft* [Living with disabilities in Angola: An ethnographic search for clues in a society injured by mines] (pp. 90). Bielefeld: Transcript.

Strauss, A. (2017). *Mirrors and masks: The search for identity*. New York: Routledge.

Suchman, L. A. (1987). *Plans and situated actions: The problem of human-machine communication*. Cambridge: Cambridge University Press.

Sutherland, E. H. (1989). *The professional thief*. Chicago: University of Chicago Press.

Svasek, M., & Domecka, M. (2012). The autobiographical narrative interview: A potential arena of emotional remembering, performance and reflection. In J. Skinner (Ed.), *The interview: An ethnographic approach* (pp. 107–126). London: Bloomsbury.

Taussig, M. (2011). *I swear I saw this: Drawings in fieldwork notebooks, namely my own*. Chicago: University of Chicago Press.

Tedlock, B. (1991). From participant observation to the observation of participation: The emergence of narrative ethnography. *Journal of Anthropological Research, 47*(1), 69–94.

Thwaites, T. (2011). *The toaster project: Or a heroic attempt to build a simple electric appliance from scratch*. New York: Princeton Architectural Press.

Tilley, C. (2009). Ethnography and material culture. In P. Atkinson, A. Coffey, S. Delamont, J. Lofland, & L. Lofland (Eds.), *Handbook of ethnography* (pp. 258–272). London: Sage.

Tilley, C., Keane, W., Kuechler-Fogden, S., Rowlands, M., & Spyer, P. (2013). *Handbook of material culture*. London: Sage.

Tondeur, K. (2016). Graphic anthropology field school: Report of a first edition. *OMERTAA Journal of Applied Anthropology*, 665–669. Retrieved August 17, 2019, from https://www.academia.edu/30888855/Graphic_Anthropology_Field_School_Report_of_a_First_Edition_2016_Omertaa_Journal_for_applied_anthropology_http_www.omertaa.org_archive_omertaa0077.pdf

Tuma, R., Schnettler, B., & Knoblauch, H. (2013). *Videographie. Einführung in die interpretative Videoanalyse sozialer Situationen* [Videography: Introduction to the interpretive video analysis of social situations]. Wiesbaden: Springer VS.

Turner, T. (1980). The social skin. In J. Cherfas (Ed.), *Not work alone: A cross-cultural survey of activities apparently superfluous to survival* (pp. 112–140). Beverly Hills: Sage.

Van Maanen, J. (2011). *Tales of the field: On writing ethnography*. Chicago: The University of Chicago Press.

Vergara, C. J. (2014). *Harlem: The unmaking of a ghetto*. Chicago: University of Chicago Press.

Vokes, R. (2007). (Re)constructing the field through sound: Actor-networks, ethnographic representation and 'radio elicitation' in south-western Uganda. In E. Hallam & T. Ingold (Eds.), *Creativity and cultural improvisation*. Oxford: Berg.

Wacquant, L. (2006). *Body & soul: Notebooks of an apprentice boxer*. Oxford: Oxford University Press.

Wang, C. C. (1999). Photovoice: A participatory action research strategy applied to women's health. *Journal of Women's Health, 8*, 185–192.

Wang, C. C., & Burris, M. A. (1997). Photovoice: Concept, methodology, and use for participatory needs assessment. *Health Education and Behavior, 24*(3), 369–387.

Whyte, W. F. (1981). *Street corner society: The social structure of an Italian slum*. Chicago: The University of Chicago Press.

Wirth, L. (1998). *The ghetto*. New Jersey: Transaction.

Yelavich, S., & Adams, B. (2014). *Design as future-making*. New York: Bloomsbury.

Zorbaugh, H. W. (1929). *Gold Coast and the slum: Sociological study of Chicago's near North Side*. Chicago: University Press.

Open Access This chapter is licensed under the terms of the Creative Commons Attribution 4.0 International License (http://creativecommons.org/licenses/by/4.0/), which permits use, sharing, adaptation, distribution and reproduction in any medium or format, as long as you give appropriate credit to the original author(s) and the source, provide a link to the Creative Commons license and indicate if changes were made.

The images or other third party material in this chapter are included in the chapter's Creative Commons license, unless indicated otherwise in a credit line to the material. If material is not included in the chapter's Creative Commons license and your intended use is not permitted by statutory regulation or exceeds the permitted use, you will need to obtain permission directly from the copyright holder.

Chapter 6
Analysis

Abstract Drawing on sociological Grounded Theory and ethnographic semantics, this chapter argues that analysis is a genuinely creative practice. Analysis entails not simply classifying the data found or produced in the field in accordance with everyday, common-sense knowledge but rather looking for aesthetic and semantic clues in it. It is also not a fixed program, but rather a hermeneutic and explorative search for new connections and patterns of meaning. This is demonstrated through examples of various data materials, such as transcripts of interviews, observation protocols, photographs, video, and material culture.

Keywords Ethnosemantic analysis · Grounded theory · Transcriptions · Visual data

Between the observation of fluid situations and their analysis there are several steps in which data is produced, sorted, assessed, discussed, and interpreted. An important question for design research is *how* this data is evaluated, whereby there is no consensus with regard to what constitutes analysis and whether doing it makes sense at all. Occasionally, design research projects conduct qualitative research and then carry out quantitative analysis (Hahn and Zimmermann 2010, p. 271). The resulting tables and pie charts may create the appearance of scientific objectivity, but it is precisely such approaches that lack an explorative engagement with the data.

Gaver et al. categorically reject analysis of Cultural Probes (1999, p. 27). This rejection of analysis is grounded in a positivistic conception of research according to which handing data in a rational way destroys its inspiring qualities. The meaning of analysis, however, is "to unbind"; it attempts to pry apart the totality of the data to find within it new combinations of meaning that are not visible at first glance. This is an interpretive and creative endeavor.

When performing analysis in the context of design research, it is useful with visual data in particular to lay these out physically in space. Photos, sketches, and illustrations—and possibly sequences of text as well—are printed out and arranged on walls and tables. Having a wide range of data facilitates cross-comparison. That is exactly what analysis is about—the search for semantic relationships, that is, similarities and differences within and outside the data. The goal consists not in prematurely classifying the data according to traditional common-sense understanding, but rather to search for new configurations of meaning within it. An analysis is an inspiring, explorative, and playful engagement with the data that is enmeshed in the iterative loops of the design process.

6.1 Transcriptions

The basis for analysis is usually text. Situations are fluid and singular and impossible to analyze because at the time of the analysis they are in the past. Every description of them is thus a linguistic reconstruction that consequently produces texts. Visual secondary data—that is photos and film—lend themselves to analysis but in the process, as soon as an interpretation is articulated, produce language as well. Ethnography can create a variety of textual forms:

- Transcriptions of interviews, conversations, and photo-elicitations
- Field notes, observation protocols, memos, and research logs
- Transcriptions of group discussions and focus groups
- Online data sets: communication strings from internet forums and chats, texts from websites, images, films
- Documents such as newspaper articles, fliers, print advertisements, annual reports, magazines
- Essays, letters, and texts from Cultural Probes and brainwriting
- Descriptions of images, film, and artifacts

Social scientific analysis takes as its basis a variety of texts, which can even consist of key words or transcribed speech sequences uttered during a photo-elicitation session or in a focus group in response to a certain artifact. Depending on the level of detail, transcription can be extremely time-intensive. Transcription software such as f4 or the Windows app Record and Transcribe reduces the amount of this effort, but producing one's own transcription can have the advantage of providing a more intensive initial engagement with the data.

The number of sequences one transcribes—whether an entire interview or only the central utterances—depends on the research questions and the context. Equally dependent on the context is the manner of the transcription. As a rule, a transcription in standard orthography—that is ordinary language—is sufficient. On the other hand, *literary transcription*, *eye dialect*, and *phonetic transcription* set down not only the content but also the prosodic features, colorations of dialect, incomprehensible expressions, and para-linguistic elements such as gestures, facial expressions, laughter, and physical movements (Kowal and O'Conell 2008, p. 441). If, for instance, the study is investigating face-to-face communication in a doctor-patient setting, then it may be important to make note of temporal overlaps in the progression of speech. It makes little sense, however, to expend enormous amounts of time writing down every clearing of the throat and every pause for thought if there is no intention to interpret these things.

Design research makes use of Grounded Theory (Brandes et al. 2009, p. 175 f.; Findeli 2004, p. 45) and ethnographic semantics (Cranz 2016, p. 6 ff.) for data analysis. Both methods correspond, more or less, to the established practice in design research of approaching data in an exploratory and open way and looking for overarching themes in it. Both methods reduce events to language (Tusting 2019), which is sometimes criticized in the context of design ethnography (Crabtree et al. 2009, p. 882).[1] As already noted, however, analysis is fundamentally based on language. This is evident in the interpretation of images. We can look at a picture and let it affect us, but as soon as we begin to interpret it and speak with someone about it, we enter the world of language, for "descriptions are always linguistic" (Eberle 2017, p. 37). And it is only when these thoughts are articulated and written down that they transcend time and space. Only then do they become intersubjectively communicable. Only then is research possible at all.

6.2 Grounded Theory

Grounded Theory was developed in the 1960s by Anselm Strauss and Barney Glaser (Bryant and Charmaz 2007; Charmaz 2014; Glaser and Strauss 1995; Holton 2018). With its interactionist, micro-sociological orientation, it presented a theoretical alternative to the structural functionalism dominant at the time. Grounded theory is not a mechanistic procedure that leads to unified, much less to objective, findings independently of the researcher; rather, the researcher actively produces data—at least in interactionist Grounded Theory.[2] Precisely *because* it leaves the researcher a great deal of freedom, Grounded Theory is a very demanding method. It does not "lead" one in a linear way through the process, but rather repeatedly makes one aware of how contingent the data is. In this regard, the method can make one uncertain. The position of Grounded Theory "is not logical; it is phenomenological" (Glaser and Strauss 1995, p. 6). Charmaz and Mitchell characterise the procedure of Grounded Theory as follows (2009, p. 160):

---

[1] Grounded Theory is also used in attempts to include non-linguistic realms, such as Geographic Information Systems (Knigge and Cope 2006) and artifacts (Lueger 2000, p. 163).

[2] In the early 1990s, the two founders of Grounded Theory had a methodological dispute with the result that today there are two variants of the method: the interactionist, pragmatic direction advocated by Anselm Strauss and the critical-rationalist version advocated by Barney Glaser. While Strauss emphasises the constructivist dimension, in which data is produced by the researcher, Glaser assumes that after theoretical saturation, certain cateogries crystalize from the data independently of the researcher. This break goes back to a short publication by Glaser "Emerging vs. Forcing. Basics of Grounded Theory" (1992), in which Glaser severely criticized Strauss (Strübing 2008, p. 65 ff.).

1. simultaneous data-collection and analysis;
2. pursuit of emergent themes through early data analysis;
3. discovery of basic social processes within the data;
4. inductive construction of abstract categories that explain and synthesize these processes;[3]
5. integration of categories into a theoretical framework that specifies causes, conditions, and consequences of these processes

The key features of Grounded Theory consist in iteration between data collection and analysis, discovery of clues in the data, ordering of the clues into categories, and the contextualization that results from this. An important element of Grounded Theory is the writing of *memos* (Charmaz and Mitchell 2009, p. 167 f.). The point here is to formulate questions and write down thoughts regarding the data, which should create a reflexive distance. These thoughts may be associative, interpretive, or speculative (Lempert 2007, p. 247). Memos are like Post-It notes. They accompany the entirety of the research process. They articulate spontaneous thoughts and associations. They are subjective without any claim to objectivity. "Memos are preliminary, partial and correctable" (Charmaz and Mitchell 2009, p. 167).

Analysis using Grounded Theory begins with open coding (Holton 2007). Open coding involves interrogating the data with questions such as "'What is the data a study of?', 'What categories does this indicate?', 'What is actually happening in the data?', 'What is the main concern being faced by the participants?' and 'What accounts for the continual resolving of this concern?'" (Glaser 1998, p. 140). Concretely, the process consists in marking the significant terms in the texts, whereby the selection criteria are of a semantic rather than a syntactic kind. The coding is applied to meanings, not to formal units such as words or sentences. Although it may be significant when a term is used frequently, the analysis is *not* about quantification. The marked codes are used as a basis for building categories. Categories are the first superordinate themes that subsume similar codes. After this, the coding proceeds further in iterative steps with increasingly greater selectivity. This multi-step coding is defined as "theoretical sampling" (Glaser and Strauss 1995, p. 45 ff.). In that regard the process of Grounded Theory resembles the funneling principle: it begins as completely open and closes in increasingly around the found concepts until theories and hypotheses grounded in the data are developed.

6.3 Ethnosemantic Analysis

A similar alternative process is ethnographic semantics or ethnosematic analysis (Spradley 1979, 1980; Maeder 1995). Here too, one begins with text, although the original text sequences are described as "native terms" (Spradley 1979, p. 73), in

---

[3]Here the method is again—as already noted—described as inductive, although it is better characterized as abduction (Strübing 2008, p. 44 ff.).

stark contrast to the "observer terms" of the ethnographer. In principle, Spradley posits: "Analysis is a search for patterns" (1980, p. 85). Ethnosemantic analysis is based on the assumption that cultural meanings are produced symbolically through language and the task consist in decoding this (Spradley 1979, p. 99).

The analysis is conducted on the basis of *native terms* (Spradley 1979, p. 73) that are specific to a particular social lifeworld. Similar terms are used to develop *domains* (Spradley 1979, p. 107 ff., 1980, p. 85 ff.). In a further step, *taxonomic analysis* (Spradley 1979, p. 132 ff., 1980, p. 112 ff.) is performed. Spradley explains this using the example of magazines: the domain "magazine" encompasses categories such as "comics," "women's magazines," or "news magazines," which are in turn broken down into "Time," "Newsweek," and "U.S. News & World Report" (1980, p. 112 ff.). Semantic connections are also investigated. Spradley mentions nine types (1979, p. 111):

1. Strict Inclusion; X is a kind of Y
2. Spatial; X is a place in Y, X is a part of Y
3. Cause-effect; X is a result of Y, X is a cause for Y
4. Rationale; X is a reason for Y
5. Location for action; X is a place for doing Y
6. Function; X is used for Y
7. Means-end; X is a way to do Y
8. Sequence; X is a step (stage) in Y
9. Attribution; X is an attribute (characteristic) of Y

In a further analytical step—known as *Componential Analysis*—individual domains are analyzed in greater depth (Spradley 1979, p. 173 ff., 1980, p. 131 ff.). Spradley explains this using the example of his daily mail, which consists of personal letters, bills, books, advertisements, etc. These categories all have their own particularities and—even before the mail is opened—they lead to certain practices and emotions. A circular will not get the same kind of attention as a personal letter with a hand-written address. A bill arouses displeasure. Which specific domains, and how many, one analyzes in depth is—as Spradley points out—a matter of discretion and depends on whether a study goes into depth or breadth (1980, p. 134). Finally, *cultural themes* are derived from the semantic relations, taxonomies, and componential analyses. These themes are "any principle recurrent in a number of domains, tacit or explicit, and serving as relationship among subsystems of cultural meaning" (Spradley 1979, p. 185 ff., 1980, p. 141).

6.4 Structured and Narrative Interviews

Expert and structured interviews are usually analyzed through content analysis. In this process, the narrative structure is broken up and the sequences are organized in accordance with the themes of the questions. Liebold and Trinczek describe this as a "top-down" logic, since the categories are already known in advance rather than generated from the data itself, as they are in Grounded Theory (2009, p. 73). This produces individual texts pertaining to different themes, the basis for which could be one or more structured or expert interviews. If there are several interviews, then commonly held and divergent positions will be compared within the individual thematic blocks.

The situation is different when theories have to be developed out of expert interviews. In that case the interview will be used to try to "tap into the interpretative knowledge of the expert—that is, to identify the principles, values, and rules that significantly shape the expert's interpretation" (Liebold and Trinczek 2009, p. 76). The coding methods of Grounded Theory are appropriate for this this "bottom-up" strategy (Liebold and Trinczek 2009, p. 76 ff.). Which variant one chooses depends not least on whether the interview was structured or open. With structured interviews, content analysis would be advantageous, while Grounded Theory would be best for open ones. Fritz Schütze proposes a six-stage analytical process for narrative interviews (1983, p. 285), in which (1) a distinction is first drawn in the text between action and interpretation. (2) The textual sequences are then described structurally. (3) The individual structural elements are analyzed and summed up in theses. (4) The behavioral patterns of the narrator, as derived from the narrative, are compared with their own ideas about their actions. (5) Then several cases are compared and (6) a theoretical model is constructed.

6.5 Computer-Based Analysis

Qualitative data can be analyzed with the help of computers using CAQDAS (Computer-Assisted Qualitative Data Analysis Software). The available programs include MAXDA, AQUAD, ATLAS.ti, MAXQDA, NVIVO, and THE ETHNOGRAPH. The coding, interpretation, and analysis is however still performed by people, while the computer programs lend support (Kuckartz 2010, p. 13). Software serves, among other things, to increase the speed of the analysis. Furthermore, codes, categories, subcategories, memos, etc. can be connected with hyperlinks, which allows for quick creation and revision of classifications. For instance, all the In-vivo codes in a particular category or all the memos on a certain topic can be activated with one click. This enables a playful approach to the data, which can continually be rearranged in new configurations.

6.6 Visual Data

First, it should be noted that while an image is an isolated entity (and can be analyzed as such), it is always produced under particular circumstances. The existence of an image is predicated on conditions that in most cases are invisible. It is produced by someone with a specific intention, possibly filtered and edited, and perhaps made

6.6 Visual Data

available to a public audience (Baur and Budenz 2017, p. 73 ff.). An important question in the analysis of visual data is whether it was produced by participants in the field or by the researcher. Photos and video produced by the researcher serve primarily as *documentation*. This is not the case for photos and videos that were produced, filtered, and edited independently of the research project within the field—for instance, party photos, selfies, Facebook profile pictures, Instagram accounts, etc. Here, it is precisely the aesthetic or the technical processing of the images that provides information about the values specific to the lifeworld, especially since these images and videos have less the function of documentation and more the quality of staging (Kirchner and Betz 2015, p. 182). In the analysis of any kind of visual material produced by the participants, there are various aspects to consider: What sort of visual material is it? What does it show? What are the conditions of its production and technical parameters? What comprises its staged qualities? What are its components? What colors dominate? What symbols are visible? What is the narrative structure or story that the image suggests? What associations does it evoke? How and where is it used? Tuma et al. posit with regard to the analysis of film—which of course applies for photos as well—that "interpretation is always a process of understanding" (Tuma et al. 2013, p. 17).

Babette Kirchner and Gregor Betz propose a hermeneutics of images rooted in the sociology of knowledge that orients itself on "natural" visual data—that is, "data considered relevant 'by the field'" (2015, p. 179), which might include photos, flyers, posters, etc. Here too the object of investigation is not just what is pictured, but rather the context in which it was produced and made public (2015, p. 184 ff.). A similar approach is advocated by Tuma et al. with *interpretative videoanalysis* (2013). There are two essential characteristics of video material that should be noted (Tuma et al. 2013, p. 33 ff.). First, its *permanence*—both in the sense that video is a permanent data recording technique in which the sequential character is chronologically preserved and in the sense that data remains permanently available. Second, its *density*—which is to say, that detailed data are produced both at the visual and auditory level. Individual sequences can also be examined and analyzed through repetition and zooming.

Data can be very heterogenous and can consist of transcribed interview sequences, observation protocols, sketches, screenshots, Facebook comments, photos, and video. Text and image data are then intertwined. Sarah Pink suggests creating linkages within the data rather than analyzing visual data separately from texts.

> [...] it involves making meaningful links between different research experiences and materials such as photography, video, field diaries, more formal ethnographic writing, participant produced or other relevant written or visual texts and other objects. These different media represent different types of knowledge and ways of knowing that may be understood in relation to one another. (Pink 2013, p. 144)

Ruth Holliday used such a process to analyze the video diaries of people in the queer scene: "Once the diaries were completed, I viewed and coded them to identify points of similarity and difference as well as recurrent themes" (2007, p. 258).

6.7 Things and Material Culture

An analysis of things is always an interpretative process—regardless of whether the things are physically present or merely depicted in photographs. In that context, Lueger and Froschauer propose four areas of artifact analysis (2018, p. 65 ff.):

- *Conditions for the artifact's existence:* How does it come about that the artifact exists at all? What historical developments are associated with the artifact? In what contexts in the social world is the artifact typically found?
- *Descriptive analysis:* What is the artifact made of? What material properties are particularly significant for the artifact? What components does it consist of? What characterizes the individual parts? What is the significance of the physical, social, and temporal contexts of the artifact?
- *Everyday contextual embedding of meaning:* What are the concepts and meanings with which the artifact is linked? Is the artifact associated with emotional and sensory qualities? What groups of actors have dealings with the artifact? How do the possible meanings ascribed to the artifact by the various groups of actors differ? To what extent is the artifact a part of everyday normality or of an extraordinary phenomenon? What are the situations in which the artifact appears?
- *Distanced structural analysis:* What are the necessary preconditions for the production of the artifact? Who has which interests connected with the production? How is the artifact produced? What are the contexts of use in which the artifact exists? How do people handle the artifact? To what extent does the way it is handled change? And to what extent does the artifact itself change? What effects are ascribed to it? What functions does it take on? To what extent does the artifact structure social settings?

These interpretive analyses should be carried out in interdisciplinary teams wherever possible. The process is particularly relevant for product design because things, function, meaning, and context are delved into in all their complex interactions. For this type of artifact analysis, Lueger suggests Grounded Theory, in which iterative loops are employed to look for structural similarities in order to verify what has been ascertained previously (2000, p. 163).

Even if explorative methods such as Grounded Theory and ethnosemantic analysis are not theoretically robust in their initial phases, the categories that result from them become associated with theories. This theoretical connection serves to reflect upon preconceived points of view and to make the findings relatable in an intersubjective frame of reference. It is based on the epistemological consideration that "neutral" observation is not possible because it is always situated and based on theoretical assumptions.

References

Baur, N., & Budenz, P. (2017). Fotografisches Handeln. Subjektive Überformung von fotografischen Repräsentationen von Wirklichkeit [Photographic action: Subjective transformation of photographic representations of reality]. In T. S. Eberle (Ed.), *Fotografie und Gesellschaft. Phänomenologische und wissenssoziologische Perspektiven* [Photography and society: Phenomenological and sociological perspectives] (pp. 73–96). Bielefeld: Transcript.

Brandes, U., Erlhoff, M., & Schemmann, N. (2009). *Designtheorie und Designforschung* [Design theory and design research]. Paderborn: Fink.

Bryant, A., & Charmaz, K. (2007). Grounded theory in historical perspective: An epistemological account. In A. Bryant & K. Charmaz (Eds.), *Handbook of grounded theory* (pp. 31–57). London: Sage.

Charmaz, K. (2014). *Constructing grounded theory*. London: Sage.

Charmaz, K., & Mitchell, R. G. (2009). Grounded theory in ethnography. In P. Atkinson, A. Coffey, S. Delamont, J. Lofland, & L. Lofland (Eds.), *Handbook of ethnography* (pp. 160–174). London: Sage.

Crabtree, A., Rodden, R., Tolmie, P., & Button, G. (2009). *Ethnography considered harmful. The status of ethnography in system design* (pp. 879–888). Boston: Association for Computing Machinery (ACM).

Cranz, G. (2016). *Ethngraphy for designers*. New York: Routledge.

Eberle, T. S. (2017). Fotografie und Gesellschaft. Theoretische Rahmung [Photography and society: Theoretical framing]. In T. S. Eberle (Ed.), *Fotografie und Gesellschaft. Phänomenologische und wissenssoziologische Perspektiven* [Photography and society: Phenomenological and sociological perspectives] (pp. 11–70). Bielefeld: Transcript.

Findeli, A. (2004). *Die projektgeleitete Forschung. Eine Methode der Designforschung* [Project-led research: A method of design research]. Swiss Design Network Symposium. HGK Basel, pp. 41–51. Retrieved May 11, 2017, from http://swissdesignnetwork.ch/src/publication/erstesdesignforschungssymposium-2004/ErstesDesignForschungssymposium_2004.pdf

Gaver, B., Dunne, T., & Pacenti, E. (1999). Cultural probes. *Interactions, 1*, 21–29.

Glaser, B. G. (1992). *Emerging vs. forcing: Basics of grounded theory*. Mill Valley, CA: Sociology Press.

Glaser, B. G. (1998). *Doing grounded theory: Issues and dicussions*. Mill Valley, CA: Sociology Press.

Glaser, B. G., & Strauss, A. L. (1995). *Discovering grounded theory: Strategies for qualitative research*. New Brunswick: Transaction.

Hahn, B., & Zimmermann, C. (2010). Visueller Atlas des Spitalalltags—Visualisierungen organisatorischer und kommunikativer Abläufe im Patientenprozess [Visual atlas of everyday hospital life: Visualizations of organizational and communicative flow in the patient process]. In C. Mareis, G. Joost, & K. Kimpel (Eds.), *Entwerfen—Wissen—Produzieren. Designforschung im Anwendungskontext* [Design—Knowledge—Production. Design research in an application context] (pp. 271–291). Bielefeld: Transcript.

Holliday, R. (2007). Performances, confessions, and identities. Using video diaries to research sexualities. In G. C. Stanczak (Ed.), *Visual research methods. Image, society, and representation* (pp. 255–305). London: Sage.

Holton, J. A. (2007). The coding process and its challenges. In A. Bryant & K. Charmaz (Eds.), *The SAGE handbook of grounded theory* (pp. 265–289). London: Sage.

Holton, J. A. (2018). From grounded theory to grounded theorizing in qualitative research. In C. Cassell, A. L. Cunliffe, & G. Grandy (Eds.), *The SAGE handbook of qualitative and business and management research methods* (pp. 233–250). London: Sage.

Kirchner, B., & Betz, G. (2015). Ethnographie und Bildhermeneutik. Visuelle Daten im Rahmen lebensweltlicher Forschung [Ethnography and hermeneutics: Visual data in the context of everyday research]. In R. Hitzler & M. Gothe (Eds.), *Ethnografische Erkundungen. Methodische Aspekte aktueller Forschungsprojekte* [Ethnographic explorations: Methodological aspects of current research projects] (pp. 177–208). Wiesbaden: Springer VS.

Knigge, L., & Cope, M. (2006). Grounded visualization: Integrating the analysis of qualitative and quantitative data through grounded theory and visualization. *Environment and Planning A, 38*, 2021–2037.

Kowal, S., & O'Connell, D. C. (2008). In U. Flick, E. von Kardorff, & I. Steinke (Eds.), *Qualitative Forschung. Ein Handbuch* [Qualitative research: A handbook] (pp. 437–447). Reinbek: Rowohlt Taschenbuch.

Kuckartz, U. (2010). *Einführung in die computergestützte Analyse qualitativer Daten* [Introduction to computer-aided analysis of qualitative data]. Wiesbaden: Springer VS.

Lempert, L. B. (2007). Asking questions of the data: Memo writing in the grounded theory tradition. In A. Bryant & K. Charmaz (Eds.), *The SAGE handbook of grounded theory* (pp. 245–264). London: Sage.

Liebold, R., & Trinczek, R. (2009). Experteninterview [Expert interview]. In S. Kühl (Ed.), *Handbuch Methoden der Organisationsforschung. Quantitative und qualitative Methoden* [Handbook of methods of organizational research: Quantitative and qualitative methods] (pp. 32–56). Wiesbaden: Springer VS.

Lueger, M. (2000). *Grundlagen qualitativer Feldforschung* [Foundations of qualitative field research]. Vienna: Vienna University.

Lueger, M., & Froschauer, U. (2018). *Artefaktanalyse. Grundlage und Verfahren* [Artifact analysis: Foundations and procedures]. Wiesbaden: Springer VS.

Maeder, C. (1995). *In totaler Gesellschaft. Eine ethnografische Untersuchung zum offenen Strafvollzug* [In total society: An ethnographic investigation into the open prison system]. Bamberg: Difo.

Pink, S. (2013). *Doing visual ethnography*. London: Sage.

Schütze, F. (1983). Biografieforschung und narratives Interview [Biography research and narrative interview]. *Neue Praxis. Kritische Zeitschrift für Sozialarbeit und Sozialpädagogik* [New Practice: Critical Journal for Social Work and Social Education], *13*, 283–293. Retrieved August 17, 2019, from https://www.ssoar.info/ssoar/bitstream/handle/document/5314/ssoar-np-1983-3-schutze-biographieforschung_und_narratives_interview.pdf

Spradley, J. P. (1979). *The ethnographic interview*. Belmont, CA: Wadsworth.

Spradley, J. P. (1980). *Participant observation*. Belmont, CA: Wadsworth.

Strübing, J. (2008). *Grounded Theory. Zur sozialtheoretischen und epistemologischen Fundierung des Verfahrens und der empirisch begründeten Theoriebildung* [Grounded theory: Toward a socio-theoretical and epistemological foundation of process and the development of empirically founded theory]. Wiesbaden: Springer VS.

Tuma, R., Schnettler, B., & Knoblauch, H. (2013). *Videographie. Einführung in die interpretative Videoanalyse sozialer Situationen* [Videography: Introduction to the interpretive video analysis of social situations]. Wiesbaden: Springer VS.

Tusting, K. (2019). *The Routledge handbook of linguistic ethnography*. London: Routledge.

Open Access This chapter is licensed under the terms of the Creative Commons Attribution 4.0 International License (http://creativecommons.org/licenses/by/4.0/), which permits use, sharing, adaptation, distribution and reproduction in any medium or format, as long as you give appropriate credit to the original author(s) and the source, provide a link to the Creative Commons license and indicate if changes were made.

The images or other third party material in this chapter are included in the chapter's Creative Commons license, unless indicated otherwise in a credit line to the material. If material is not included in the chapter's Creative Commons license and your intended use is not permitted by statutory regulation or exceeds the permitted use, you will need to obtain permission directly from the copyright holder.

Chapter 7
Representation and Reporting

Abstract Design needs language and text so that it can be negotiated intersubjectively and become capable of connection to other academic disciplines. Texts, however, do not objectively reflect realities but rather bring them forth through their own medium: academic, journalistic, essayistic, and literary texts afford very particular ways of viewing the world. Scientific truths are produced narratively as well—at least from the constructivist perspective. This is particularly the case for the texts of design ethnography, in which a story-telling quality is inherent and which may take on subjectivist perspectives. These aspects of design ethnography must be consciously reflected in the process.

Keywords Language · Subjectivity · Story · Transmission · Writing culture

The French author Raymond Queneau, like Georges Perec a representative of the "OuLiPo" movement, published a little book in the 1960s called *Exercises in Style* (2012). In it, he tells a story about seeing a man on a bus in Paris who is annoyed because he is repeatedly jostled by his neighbor. Two hours later, the same man is standing on a city square where a colleague points out to him that he needs to have a button sewn onto his coat. The story is called "Notation" (2012, p. 3). It is insignificant and trivial. The book then offers 98 more versions of "the same" story, but told in a variety of narrative forms. Queneau tells the story as "Retrograde," "Dream," "Negativism," "Philosophic," "Biased," etc. What is the author trying to tell us with all this? It is not *one* story, told in 99 variations, but rather 99 stories. With each new version, the sentences produce a different reality. It is not possible to tell the story in a "neutral" form. Of course, one can attempt it—only then this version would take its place next to the others as "Neutral." In that respect, there is no such thing as a linguistic description of an objective reality: "Through his choice of words and method of organization, a writer presents a version of the world. As a selective and creative activity, writing always functions more as a filter than a mirror reflecting the 'reality' of events" (Emerson et al. 1995, p. 66).

A certain text creates a certain reality. We intuitively realize whether we are reading a scientific, essayistic, journalistic, or literary text—and have corresponding expectations. That we realize this is not only due to the text itself, but is already guided by the medium: We have different expectations when we are holding an anthropological journal or a literary novel in our hands. We read the *New York Times* differently than a tabloid, a blog differently than an SMS. Haptic, creative, typographic, visual, linguistic, and contextual factors play a role in this framing.

Epistemological questions of this kind have been addressed by anthropology in the "writing culture" debate. Ethnographic accounts, it is argued, do not represent reality but rather bring it forth (Clifford and Marcus 1986; Geertz 1988; van Maanen 1995). Accordingly, ethnographic findings are not objective, but rather narratively produced and partial (Adler and Adler 2012; Clifford 1986, p. 7; Emerson et al. 1995, p. 3). They are *Tales of the Field* (van Maanen 2011). Language objectifies an observed, fluid situation that, at the time of the description, is irreversibly in the past. What is objectified is not observed reality, but *only* the text. When we write texts, we are relying on conventions. We can play with these conventions—partially break them, the way the OuLiPo writers attempt—but we cannot eliminate them entirely because language itself is a convention. How findings are linguistically "told" depends on the context of the project and the methodological approaches with which the research was conducted and documented. If there was video produced in the field, it can be made into an ethnographic documentary film. The same film material can be analyzed linguistically, through which it is then transferred into another form. Or sketches, for instance, could be employed either for documentation or as a memory aid, but they could also be a form in which to convey insights. The great extent to which transmission formats can vary is exemplified by the Japanese artist Tatsuo Inagaki, who conducted interviews in an iterative process with people from troubled neighborhoods in Mexico City and Antalya, Turkey and then turned the results into museum installations that were exhibited to the public, with whom he then engaged in dialog. He subsequently conducted workshops and readings with the people in local contexts. The results were then put together in documentaries (Inagaki 2010, p. 76 ff.).

What form of transmission is chosen depends on the goals of the project and the context. In the case of a course of study at an art college, the context is usually that a written thesis must be produced to graduate. This may sometimes be criticized as "academicization," but engagement with epistemological and methodological questions is what makes design capable of interdisciplinary connection, enabling it to have greater impact on other disciplines. This is only possible through language. Even the interpretation of an image becomes communicable and intersubjectively accessible only after it is linguistically negotiated (Poferl and Keller 2017, p. 314). It is an illusion to believe that design can do without language. It is precisely the interdisciplinary position of design that requires it to enable the sort of communicative connections that are only possible through language.

In contrast to ethnography in the social sciences, the way in which findings are ultimately worked up in the context of design is more variable and depends largely on the goals of the research project: "[. . .] there is no one 'natural' or 'correct' way to write about what one observes" (Emerson et al. 1995, p. 5). When a student conducts ethnographic research, the notes serve as the basis for an ethnographic report that is integrated into a theoretical thesis. Such a thesis must meet formal requirements that differ from the research documentation. The documentation reflects the research process more or less chronologically. In the thesis, however, a new structure is created that follows an intrinsic logic specific to the research (Cranz 2016, p. 113 ff.).

References

Adler, P., & Adler, P. (2012). Tales from the field: Reflections on four decades of ethnography. *Qualitative Sociological Review, 8*(1), 11–32.
Clifford, J. (1986). Introduction: Partial truths. In J. Clifford & G. E. Marcus (Eds.), *Writing culture: The poetics and politics of ethnography* (pp. 1–26). Los Angeles: University of California Press.
Clifford, J., & Marcus, G. E. (1986). *Writing culture: The poetics and politics of ethnography*. Los Angeles: University of California Press.
Cranz, G. (2016). *Ethngraphy for designers*. New York: Routledge.
Emerson, R. M., Fretz, R. I., & Shaw, L. L. (1995). *Writing ethnographic fieldnotes*. Chicago: University of Chicago Press.
Geertz, C. (1988). *Works and lives: The anthropologist as author*. Stanford: Stanford University Press.
Inagaki, T. (2010). Fieldwork as artistic practice. In A. Schneider & C. Wright (Eds.), *Between art and anthropology: Contemporary ethnographic practice* (pp. 75–81). New York: Bloomsbury.
Poferl, A., & Keller, R. (2017). Die Wahrheit der Bilder [The truth of the pictures]. In T. S. Eberle (Ed.), *Fotografie und Gesellschaft. Phänomenologische und wissenssoziologische Perspektiven* [Photography and society: Phenomenological and sociological perspectives] (pp. 305–315). Bielefeld: Transcript.
Queneau, R. (2012). *Exercises in style*. New York: New Directions Books.
Van Maanen, J. (1995). *Representation in ethnography*. London: Sage.
Van Maanen, J. (2011). *Tales of the field: On writing ethnography*. Chicago: University of Chicago Press.

Open Access This chapter is licensed under the terms of the Creative Commons Attribution 4.0 International License (http://creativecommons.org/licenses/by/4.0/), which permits use, sharing, adaptation, distribution and reproduction in any medium or format, as long as you give appropriate credit to the original author(s) and the source, provide a link to the Creative Commons license and indicate if changes were made.

The images or other third party material in this chapter are included in the chapter's Creative Commons license, unless indicated otherwise in a credit line to the material. If material is not included in the chapter's Creative Commons license and your intended use is not permitted by statutory regulation or exceeds the permitted use, you will need to obtain permission directly from the copyright holder.

Chapter 8
Epilogue

Abstract Design ethnography consists in iterative processes in which research, interventions, and design flow into one another, whereby design itself develops epistemological qualities. Design ethnography means moving rapidly between the various approaches and constantly adopting new perspectives. Methods should not be dogmatically adhered to, but can and should be adapted and transcended. Design ethnography is therefore a "dirty" practice that tends toward anarchy. It can become "clean" and intersubjectively accessible only by means of inner distancing, conscious reflection, and not least, language.

Keywords Design intervention · Engaged action · Iteration · Materialization · Reflection

In design ethnography, research, intervention, and design are intertwined in iterative processes (Otto and Smith 2013, p. 11) and practice is reflected upon theoretically and methodologically. Reflection takes place when something is articulated in language, which is a form of translation. Because language generalizes, something gets lost in this translation—namely, the intrinsic and ineffable understanding of praxis. At the same time, something is gained—namely, reflection and the possibility of intersubjective connection.

To capture one's own actions in language implies the kind of distancing that is typical of reflection. The practices and research methods of design ethnography are variable and diverse—and should be well-founded and consciously considered. Only in this way can design research become a discipline that has impact on other disciplines and enters into dialogue and exchange with them. Only through the articulation and explication of the process can methods be developed that can be applied, changed, expanded, transcended, and adapted. A method isn't simply fixed and self-contained—rather, it is an ongoing process (Crabtree et al. 2012, p. 67; Salvador et al. 1999, p. 41). Due to the playful and iterative approaches inherent in design practice, design ethnography has a high potential for methodological innovation (Otto and Smith 2013, p. 11 ff.) that is also interesting and inspiring for cultural anthropology and sociology.

Reflecting on methods in the context of design ethnography thus means considering practice (Schön 1983), which changes the role of the ethnographer. While in cultural sociology and anthropology, the ethnographer leads a "strange double life" (Maeder 2008, p. 251) between active participation and internal distancing, designers alter what happens in the field through intervention. It is not just passive observation but also engaged action that leads to insight (Maturana and Varela 2003, p. 13). It may be concluded that these design techniques do not just objectivize previously generated knowledge, but "that designing must be seen as a cognitive process that produces knowledge" (Ammon and Froschauer 2013, p. 16). This implies that designers switch quickly and in response to the situation between roles and perspectives. They switch between giving form and doing research, between active intervention and passive observation. They transfer findings into hypotheses and materializations, such as prototypes. The potential of design ethnography, which is not (nor can it be) a self-contained method, consists in rapid transfers of images into words and of words into designs, the application of which is in turn reflected upon and articulated. It consists in quick and situational changes between thinking styles and perspectives, in a restless search for cosmologies of reality and the interventions that alter them.

References

Ammon, S., & Froschauer, E. M. (2013). Zur Einleitung: Wissenschaft Entwerfen. Perspektiven einer reflexiven Entwurfsforschung [An introduction: Designing science. Perspectives of reflexive design research]. In S. Ammon & E. M. Froschauer (Eds.), *Wissenschaft Entwerfen: Vom forschenden Entwerfen zur Entwurfsforschung der Architektur* [Designing science: From researching design to design research in architecture] (pp. 15–44). Munich: Wilhelm Fink.

Crabtree, A., Roucefield, M., & Tolmie, P. (2012). *Doing design ethnography*. London: Springer.

Maeder, C. (2008). Sehen, aber nicht schauen [Seeing but not looking]. In F. Sutterlüty & P. Imbusch (Eds.), *Abenteuer Feldforschung. Soziologen erzählen* [Adventures in field research: Stories from sociologists] (pp. 251–256). Main: Campus.

Maturana, H. R., & Varela, F. J. (2003). *El árbol del conocimiento. Las bases biológicas del entendimiento humano* [The tree of knowledge: The biological basis of human understanding]. Buenos Aires: Lumen.

Otto, T., & Smith, R. C. (2013). Design anthropology: A distinct style of knowing. In W. Gunn, T. Otto, & R. C. Smith (Eds.), *Design anthropology: Theory and practice* (pp. 1–29). London: Bloomsbury.

Salvador, T., Bell, G., & Anderson, K. (1999). Design ethnography. *Design Management Journal, 10*(4), 35–41. https://doi.org/10.1111/j.1948-7169.1999.tb00274.x.

Schön, D. A. (1983). *The reflexive practitioner: How professionals think in action*. New York: Basic Books.

Open Access This chapter is licensed under the terms of the Creative Commons Attribution 4.0 International License (http://creativecommons.org/licenses/by/4.0/), which permits use, sharing, adaptation, distribution and reproduction in any medium or format, as long as you give appropriate credit to the original author(s) and the source, provide a link to the Creative Commons license and indicate if changes were made.

The images or other third party material in this chapter are included in the chapter's Creative Commons license, unless indicated otherwise in a credit line to the material. If material is not included in the chapter's Creative Commons license and your intended use is not permitted by statutory regulation or exceeds the permitted use, you will need to obtain permission directly from the copyright holder.

The manufacturer's authorised representative in the EU is Springer Nature Customer Service Centre GmbH, Europaplatz 3, 69115 Heidelberg, Germany. If you have any concerns regarding our products, please contact ProductSafety@springernature.com

Printed and bound by CPI Group (UK) Ltd, Croydon, CR0 4YY

25/03/2026

02078197-0010